JASON NOCITO

LOADS

INTRODUCTION BY
ALI SUBOTNICK

A TINYVICES BOOK

aperture

THE MAN WHO SHOT THE WORLD

ALI SUBOTNICK

I have rarely seen him without a lens attached to his face. Actually, I am pretty sure that I have never seen his face. I am convinced that he doesn't have real eyes, but uses the camera so he can look at the world. And the camera filters out the boring, glaring noise so that when we see the world through Jason Nocito's eyes it is clear and focused, sad and beautiful, strange and wrong, sexy and dirty, confusing and right.

It started when he was a young boy, an orphan living on the streets of Idaho, wandering on his tricycle looking for a hot meal and a warm coat. Then he was taken in by a gracious elder who had a tape recorder where his right ear should be so he could process all he heard into soundtracks for life. This old man showed Jason how to live as a half-man/half-machine without becoming a freak show or a science experiment. The wise man taught him how to take in and make sense of all the chaos and despair around him by exploiting disorder and zeroing in on the minutiae of these frenetic moments. Jason eventually moved to the big city where he'd ride his tricycle around town capturing the pictures whizzing by.

He takes a lot of photographs of people, but they are often hidden by a shadow or are obstructed by something, a tree, a person. Sometimes they cover their faces. Maybe Jason-the-Camera-Man has only one working eye so he squints, shoots, and captures portraits that reveal just a hint of a person. I think it is partly his way of reassuring himself that even though he has this camera-face, he is still a whole person. He reveals characters that feel overlooked. At times, they appear to be lonely and lost, or deranged and disgusting.

Some of his pictures are so abstract that you cannot even recognize what's being depicted. You cannot figure out why he took a picture of that cassette tape or that wood grain. And what's up with all the lists? He sees a lot of really banal stuff: a jelly donut, a classroom full of chairs, an air conditioner, an office light fixture. Daisies blowing so hard in the wind they are beyond broken. A nasty plate of something posing as meat, reflected in a mirror on a dingy tile counter. If his camera sees something gross like that, does it eat it? Probably. It eats it and then shits it out as a photo. That upside down clown mask is just plain scary, and that fork? Some old guy is watching a fire burning in a fireplace– on TV. There's a house totally covered in ivy; all you can see is a shingled roof.

Even his landscapes are off. There are fog, big rocks, trees, and desolate nature–ideal environments to get lost inside your head. Maybe Jason goes to these places to get lost, or maybe he is lost and uses the camera to find his way out. And then he wound up in that spooky cabin in the woods all covered in ivy–thinking he would make it to the one with the light on . . .

In his photos, things are in places they don't belong or you would never think to find them. I bet the camera finds things for him. It probably has some sort of alien chip inside of it that zeroes in on invisible things. The back of a head. A crack in the sidewalk. A stain on a couch. A snowy day, a snow globe. A sign on the road. A stack of books. A TV antenna. A spill on the stairs. It's all equalized and interchangeable, but sometimes the pieces don't fit.

We never get the whole picture. There is always something missing, and those gaps emphasize things we would probably never notice. They make you want to scream and kick and crawl out of the muck, or dive back in and hide. Jason-the-Camera-Man focuses on insignificant details, strange angles, and weird juxtapositions of things that should not be seen together. Ever. But in his world they make sense. It is as if the way we see without his lens is misguided and fuzzy and out of focus. He cleans up the world, clarifies our confusion, and then he makes it messy and scary again. He wants us to cry and love and kill ourselves and thrive. It is the end and just the beginning.

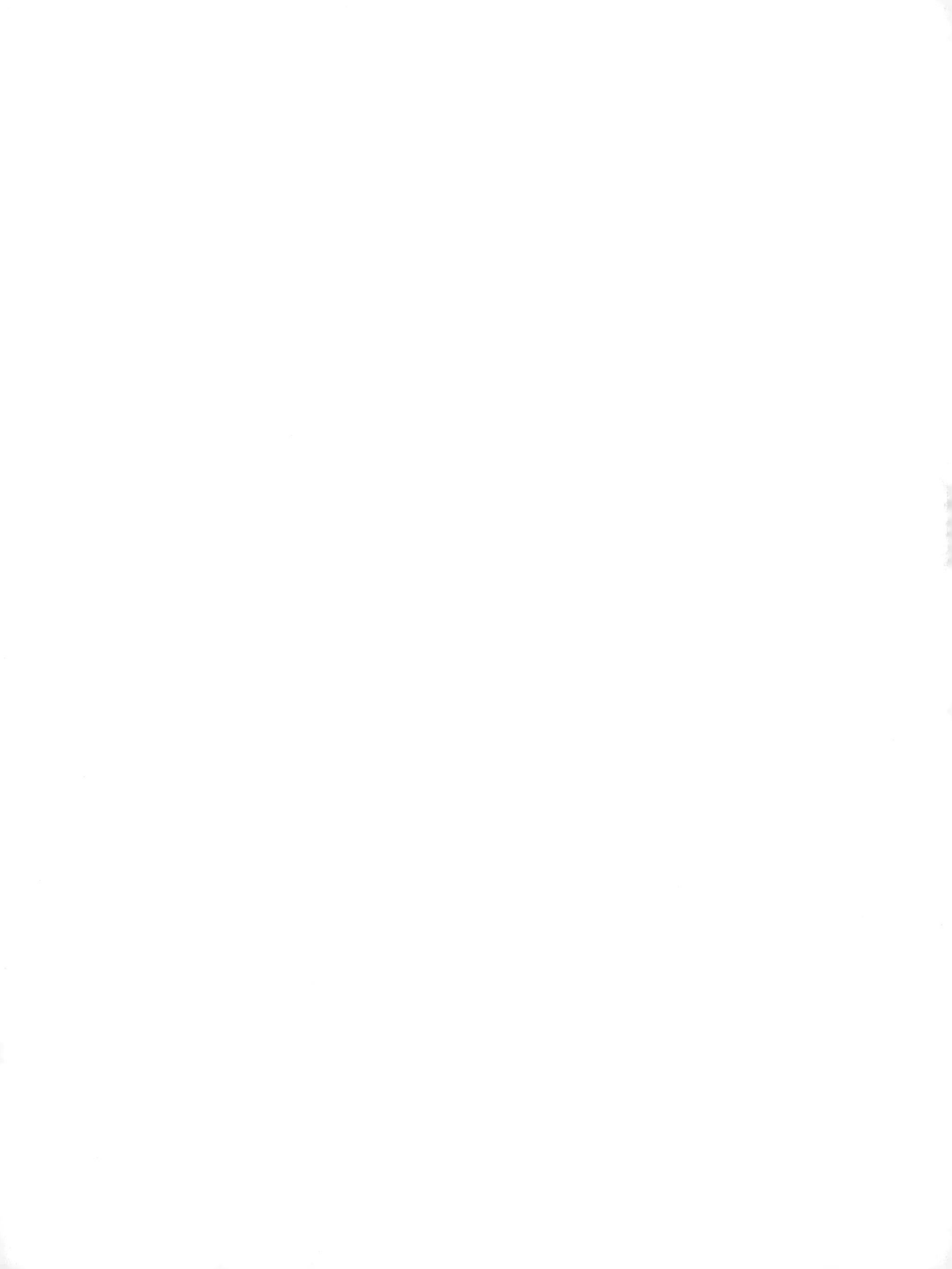

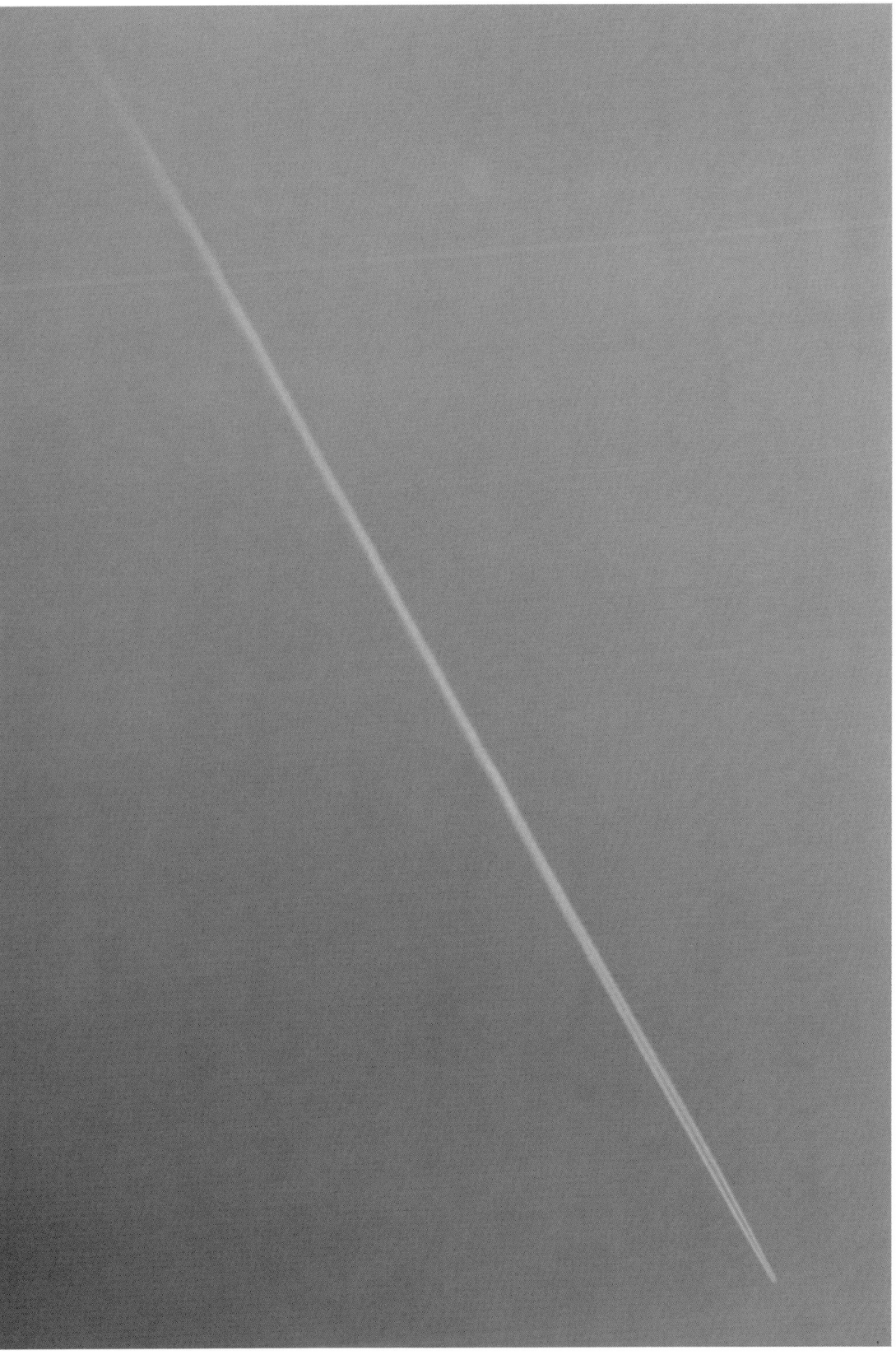

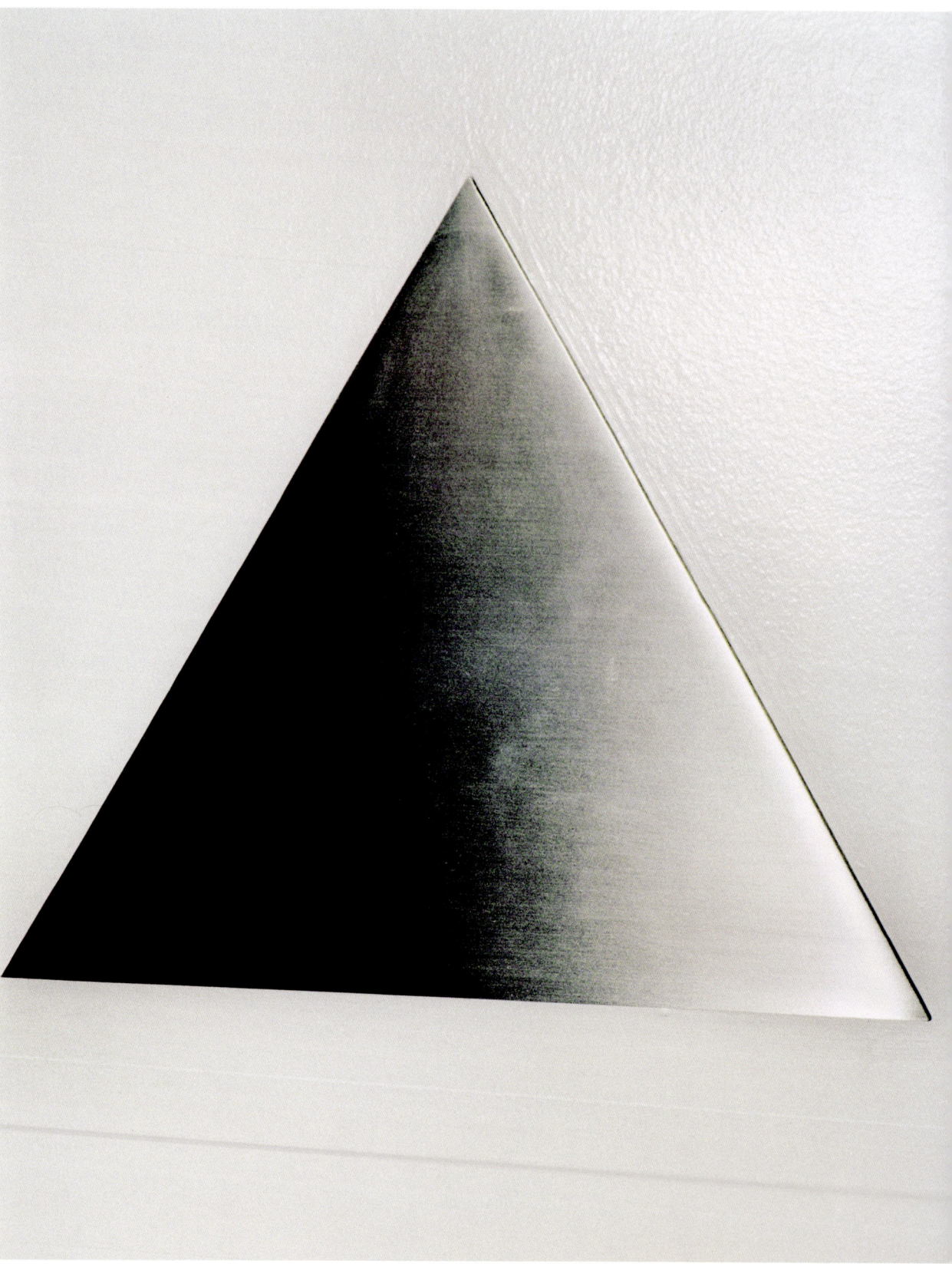

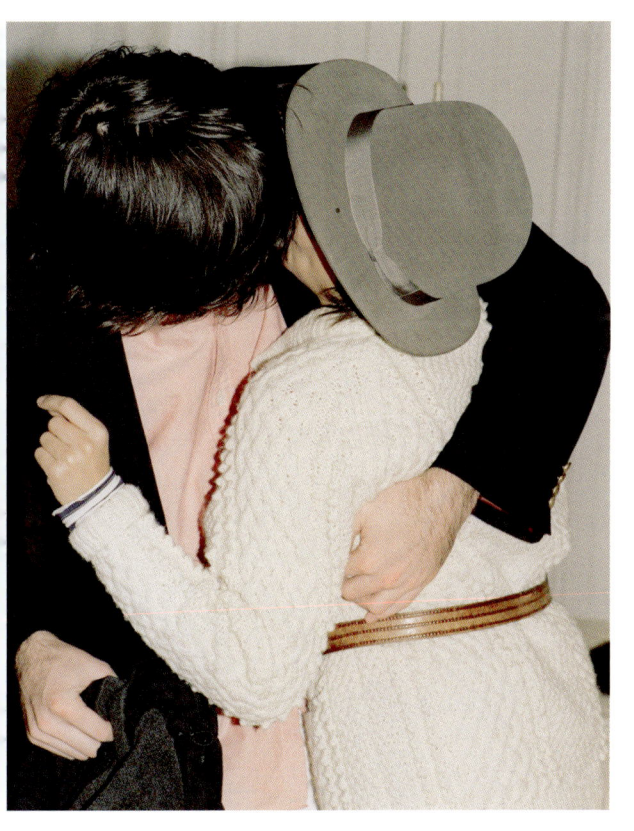

Throughout the
performance,
this production
will utilize
pyrotechnics,
strobe lights,
and fog devices.

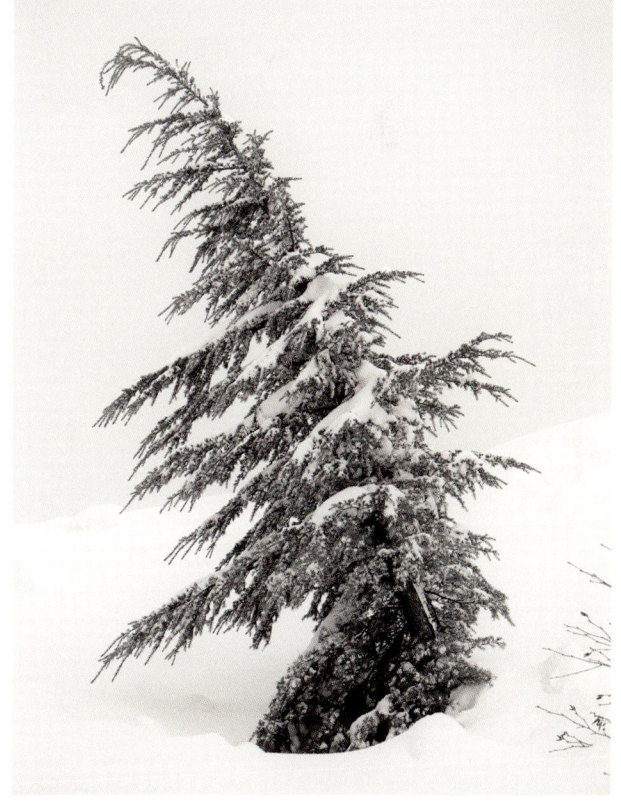

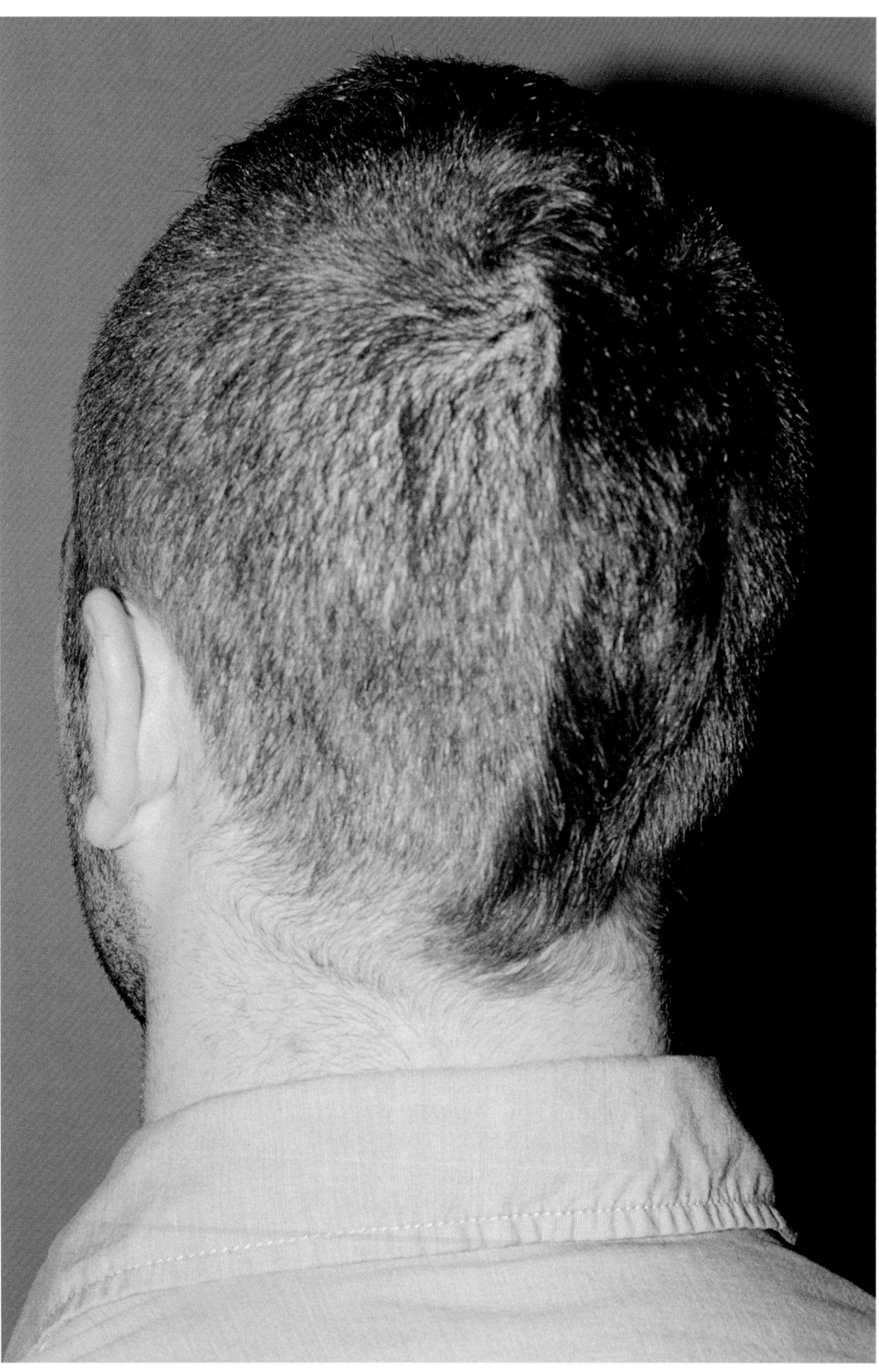

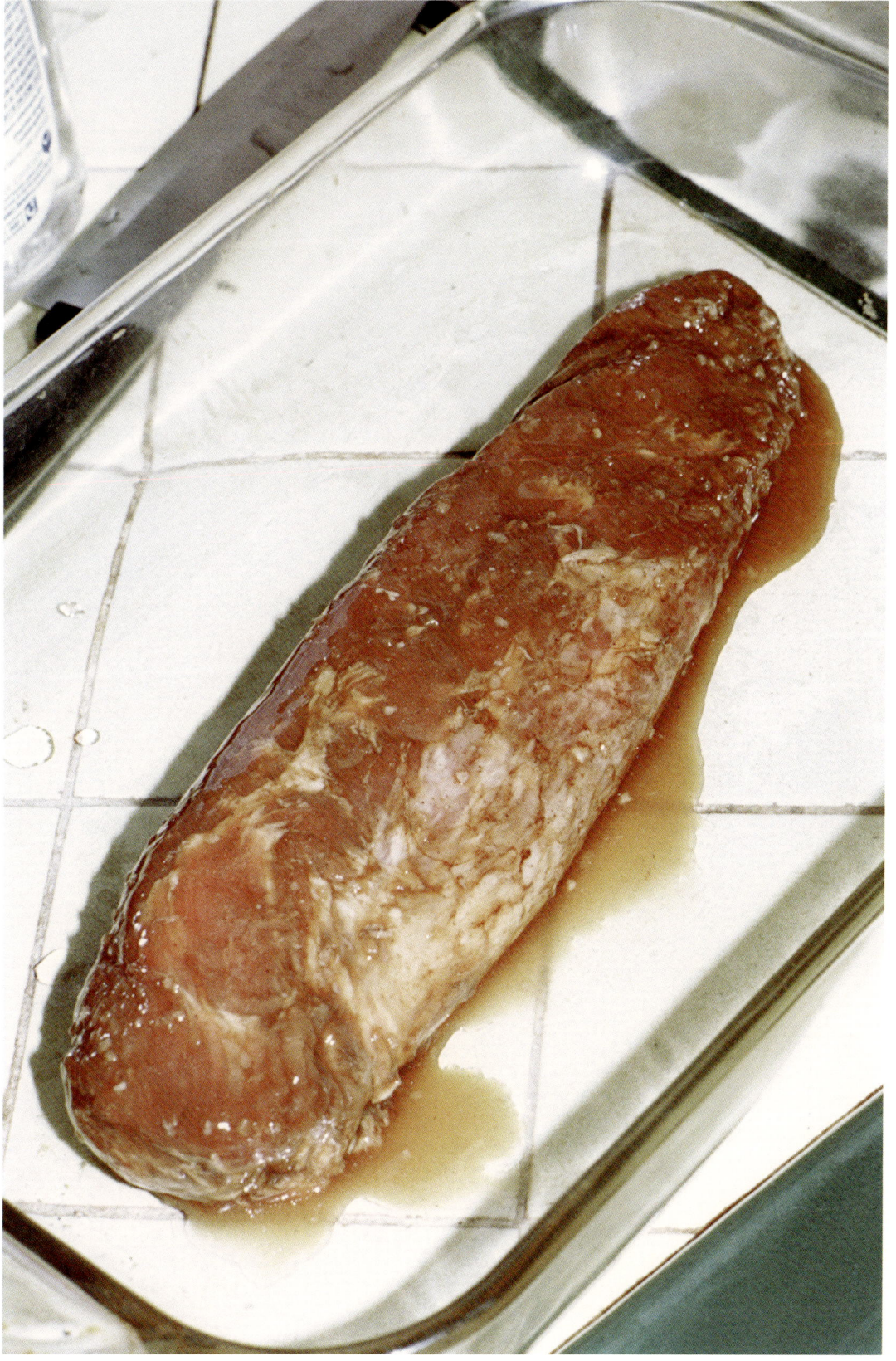

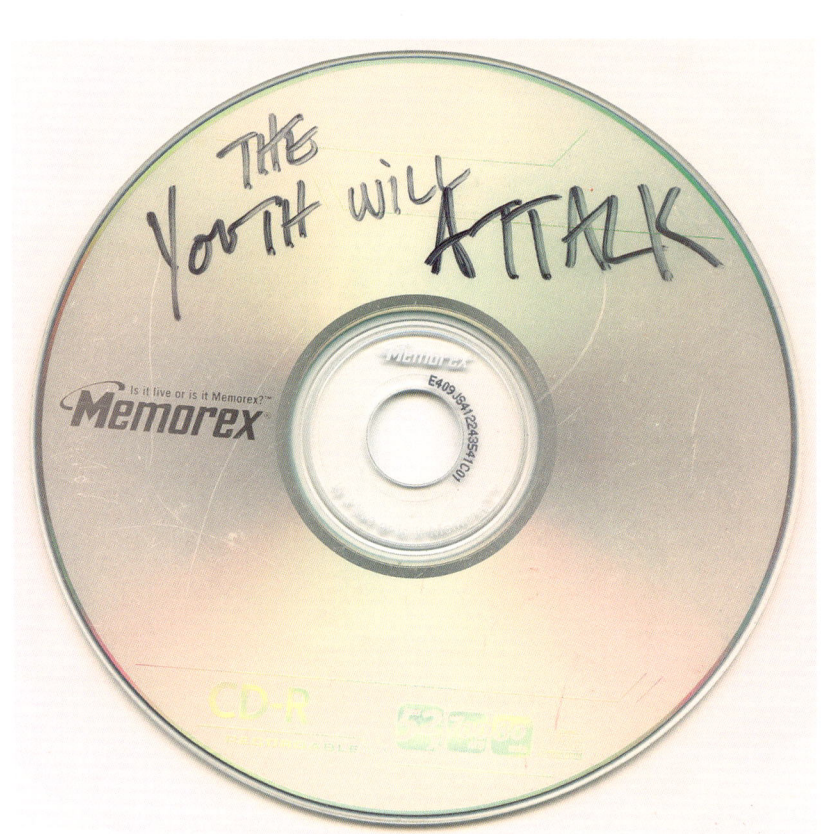

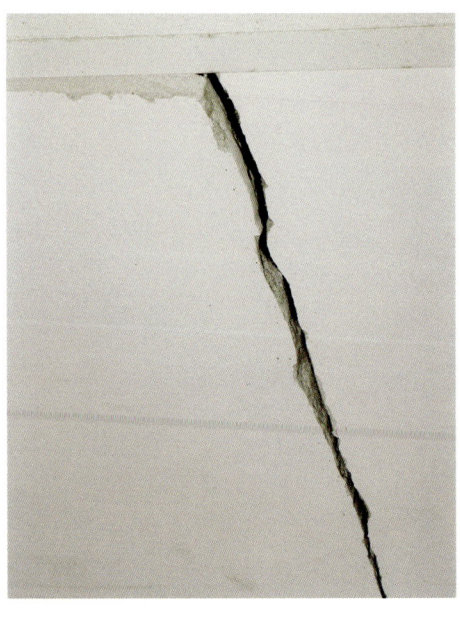

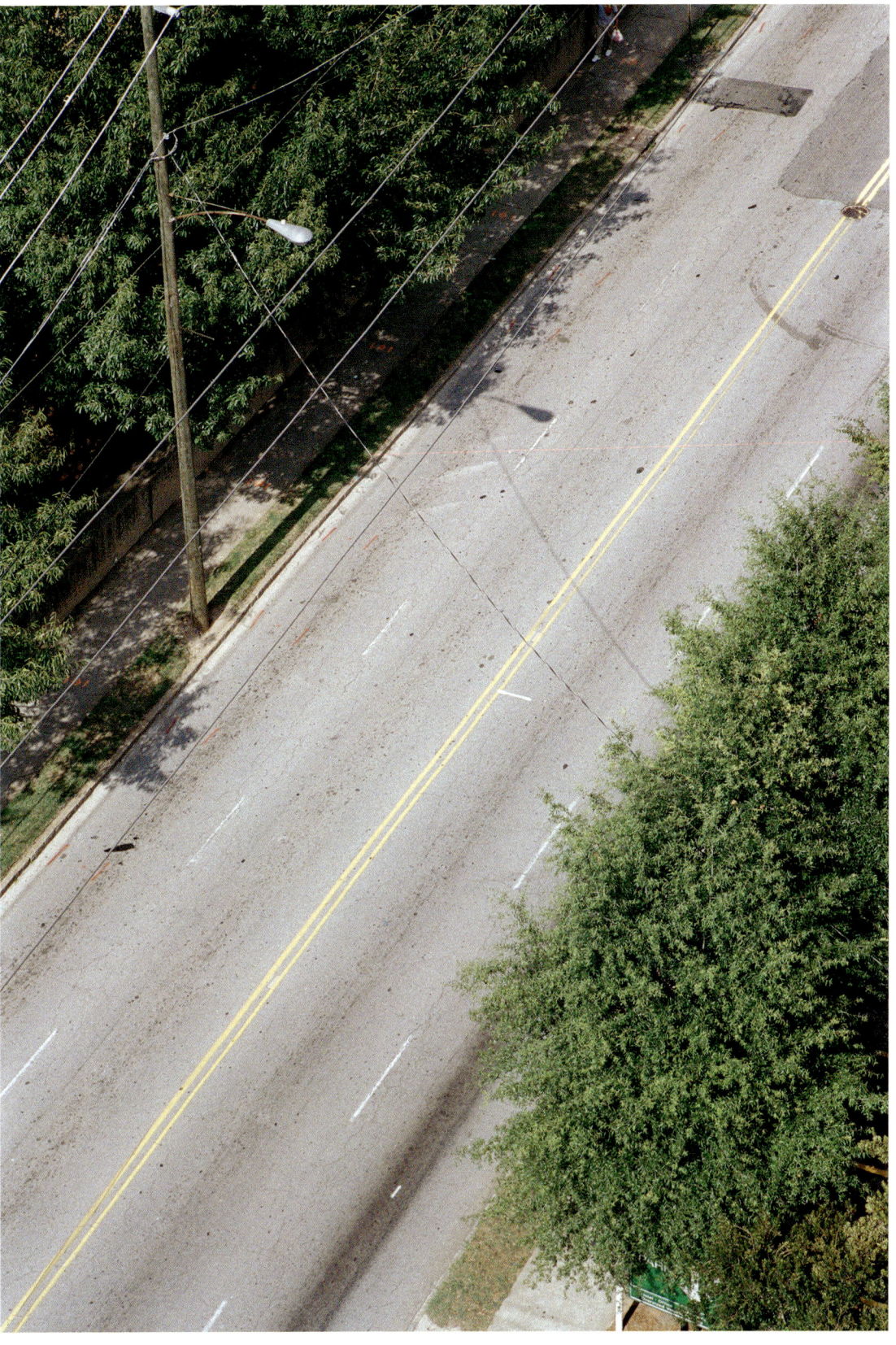

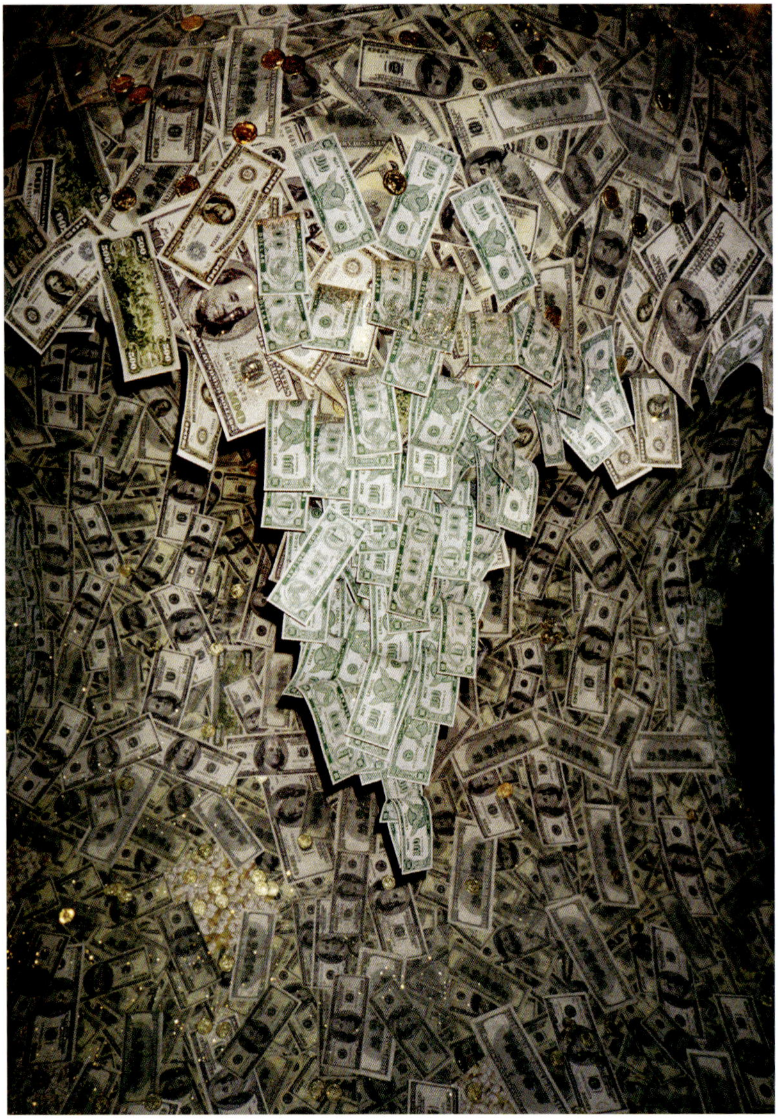

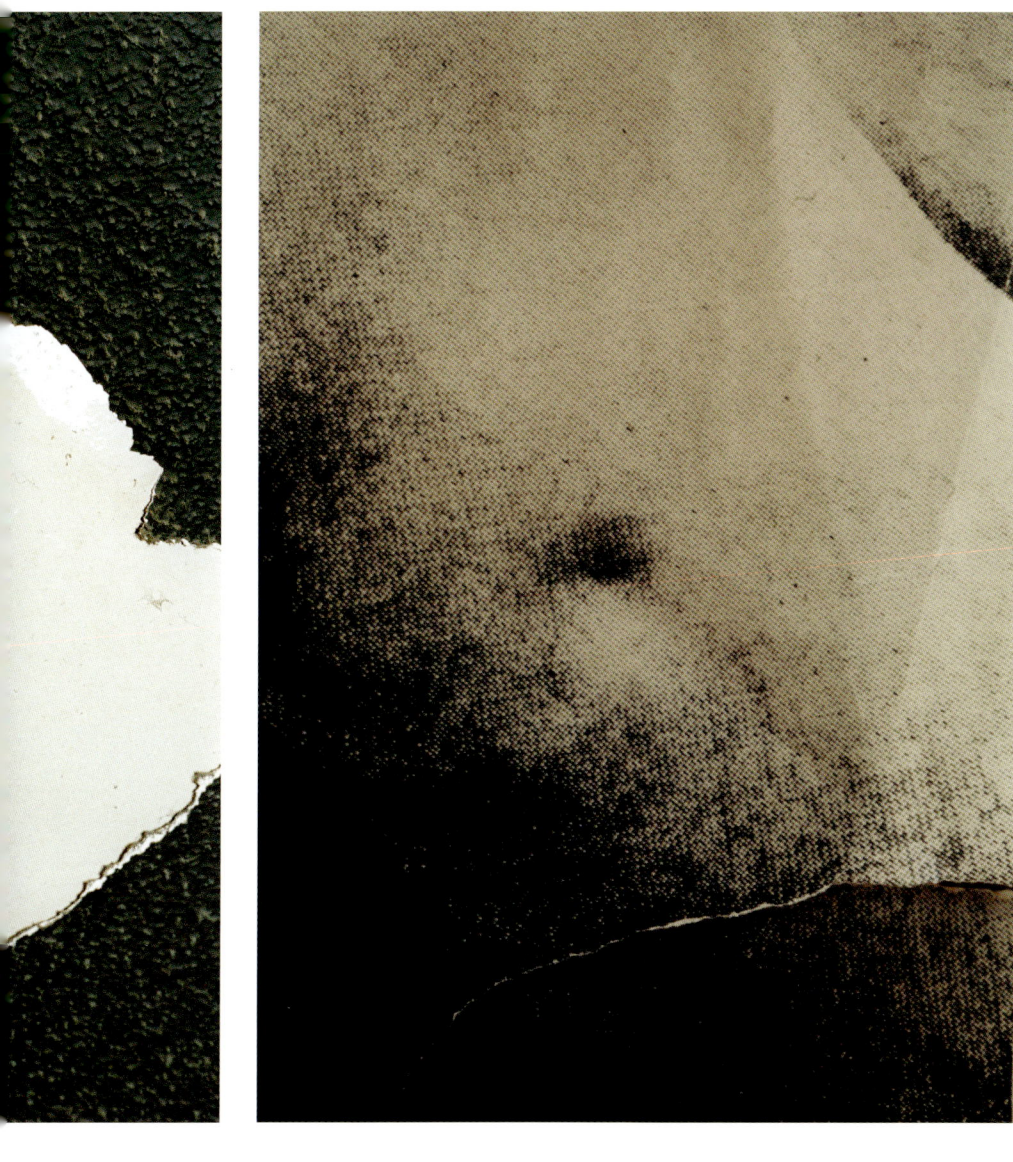

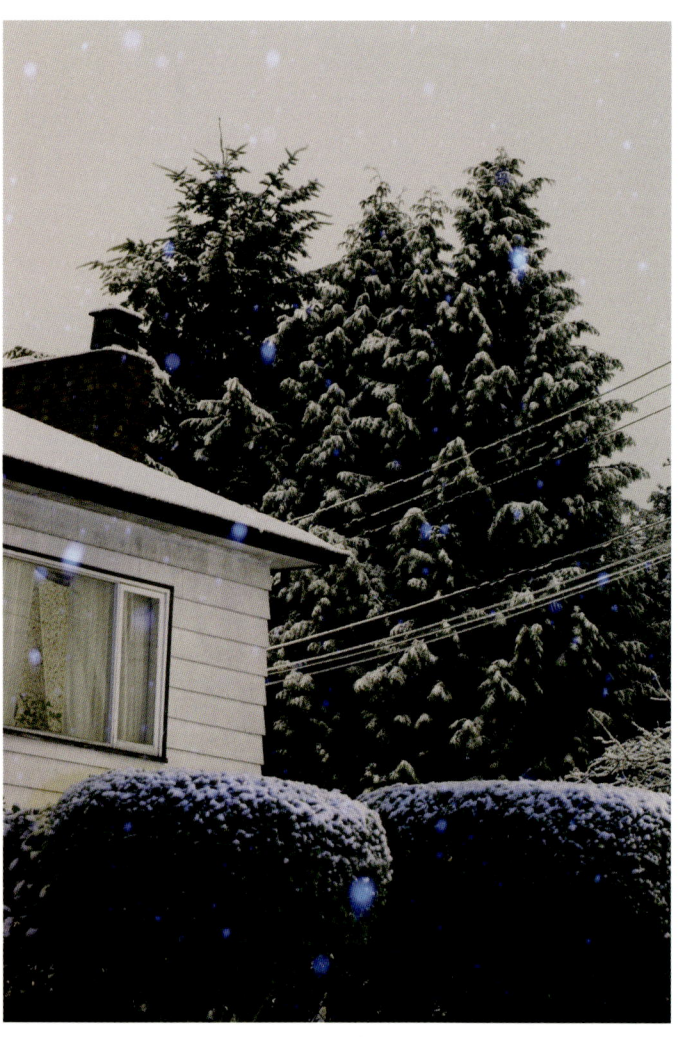

Home Again
At Home Again
Back Home Again
Home Again, 1952
Home Again Blues
Come Home Again
Down Home Again
Home Again to You
Home Again With You
Back to Home Again
Home Again and Free
Coming Home Again
Comin' Home Again
Home Again Polka
Home Alone Again

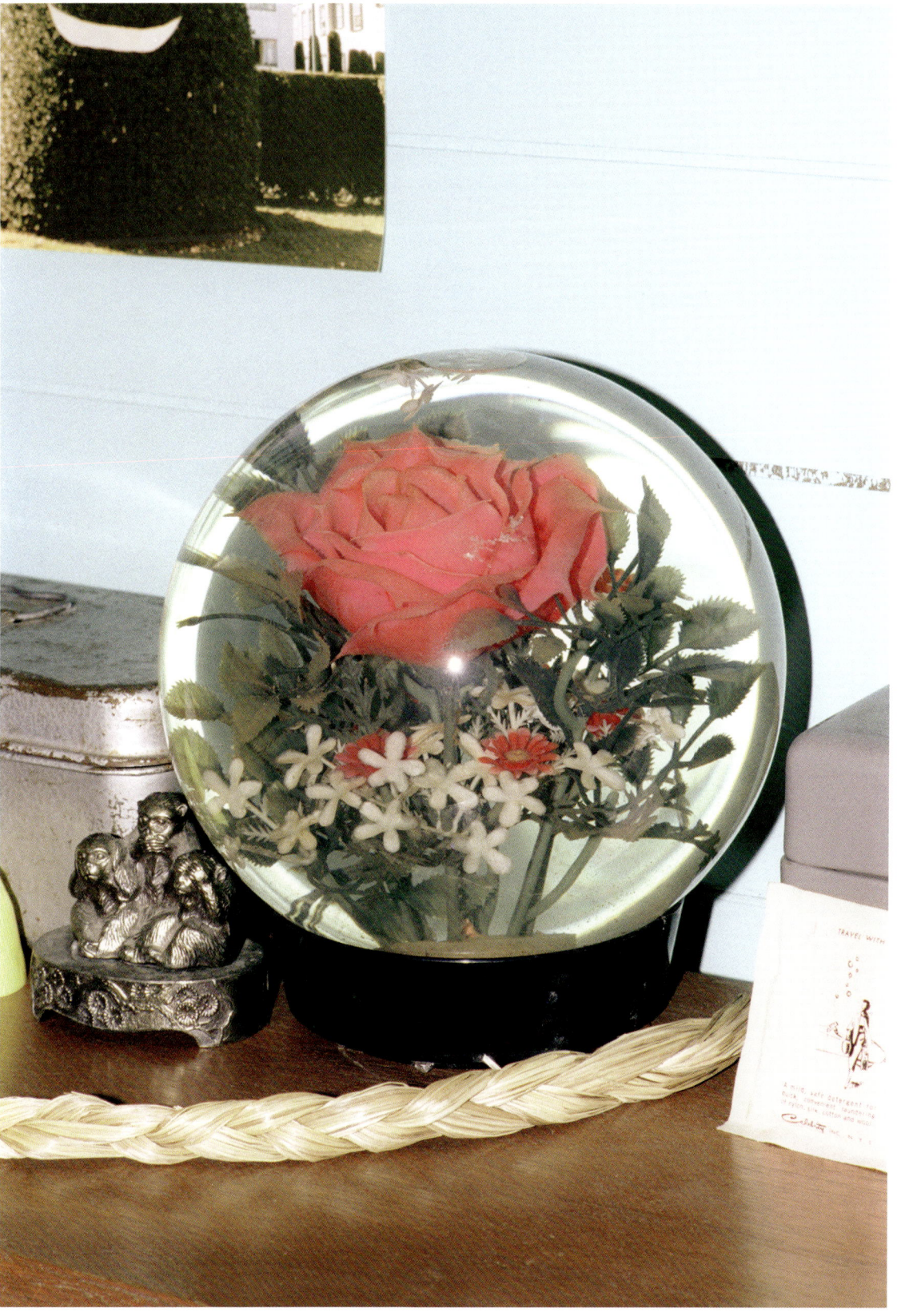

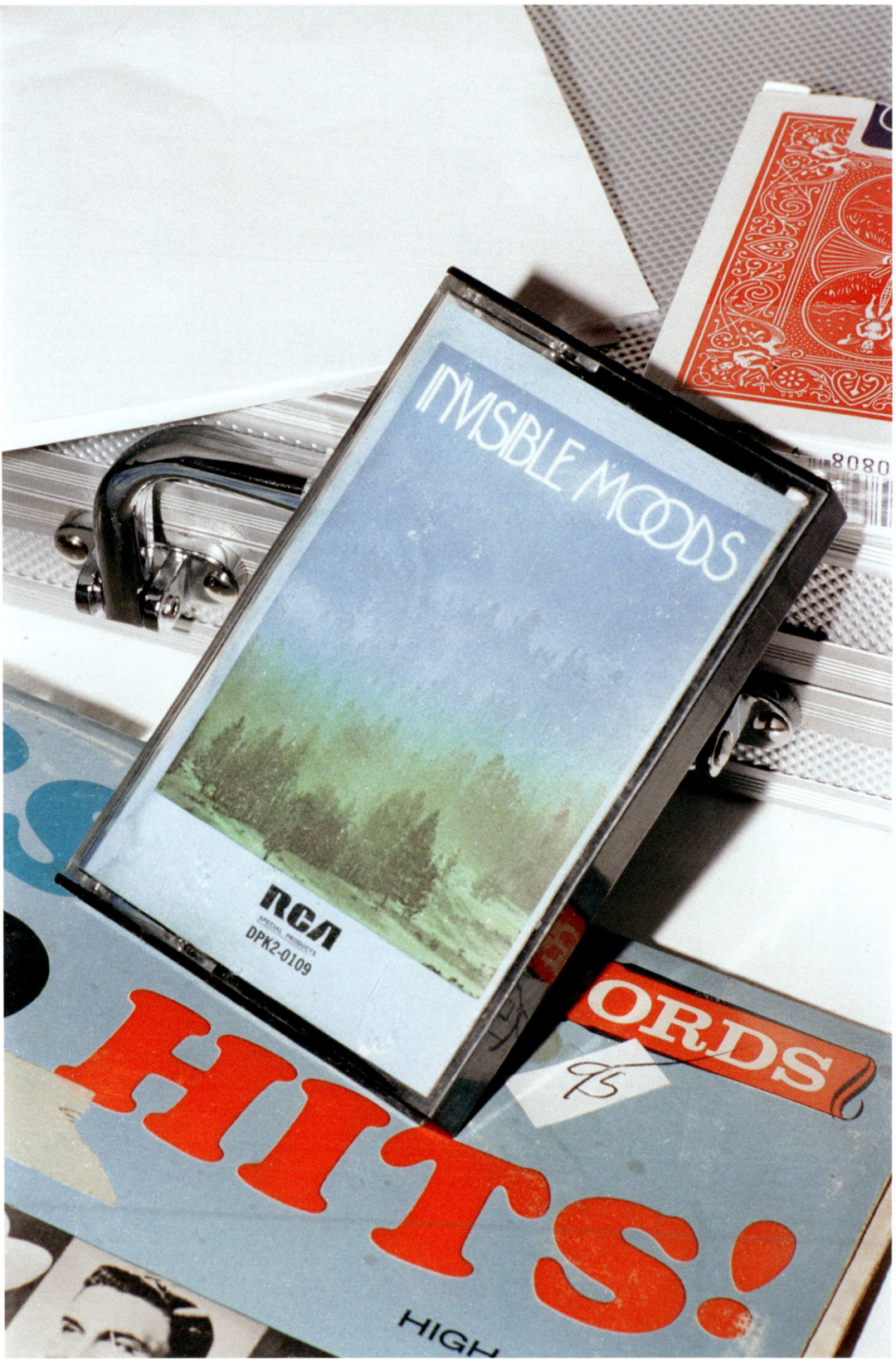

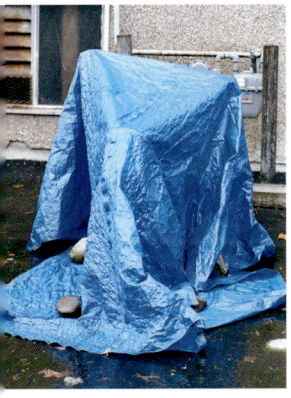

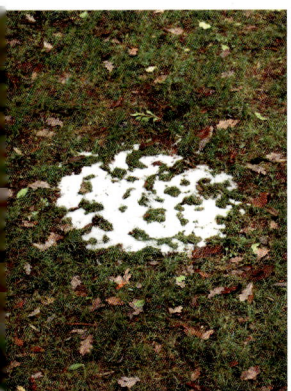

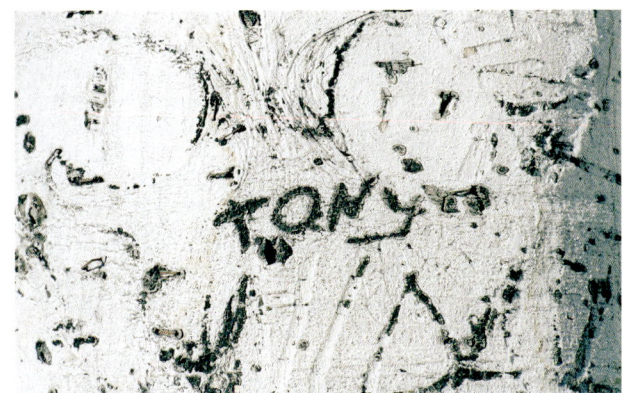

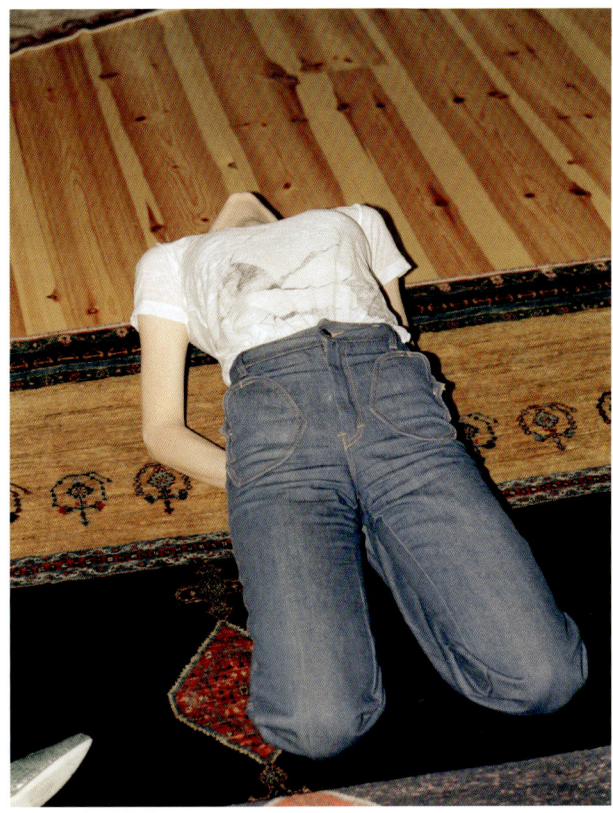

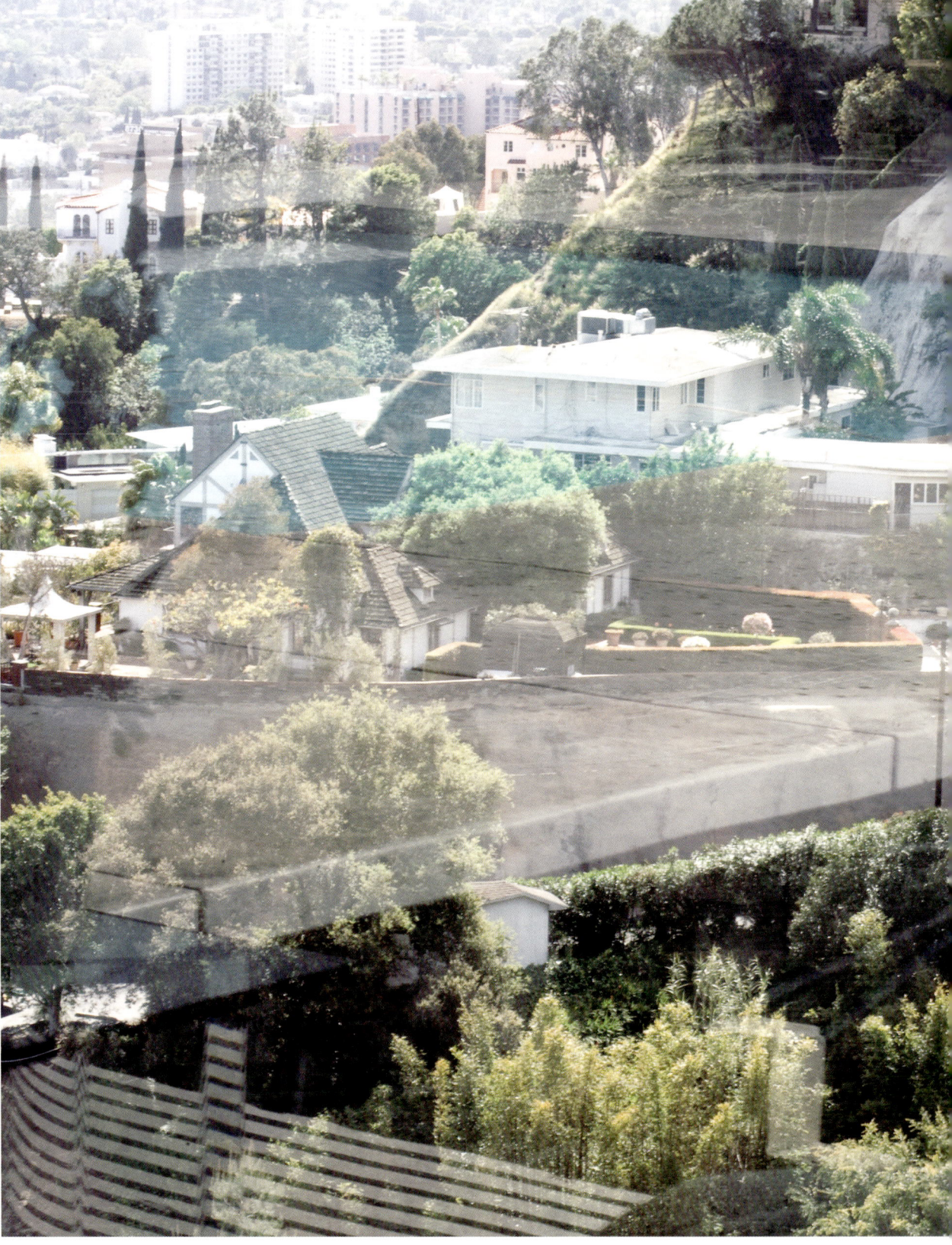

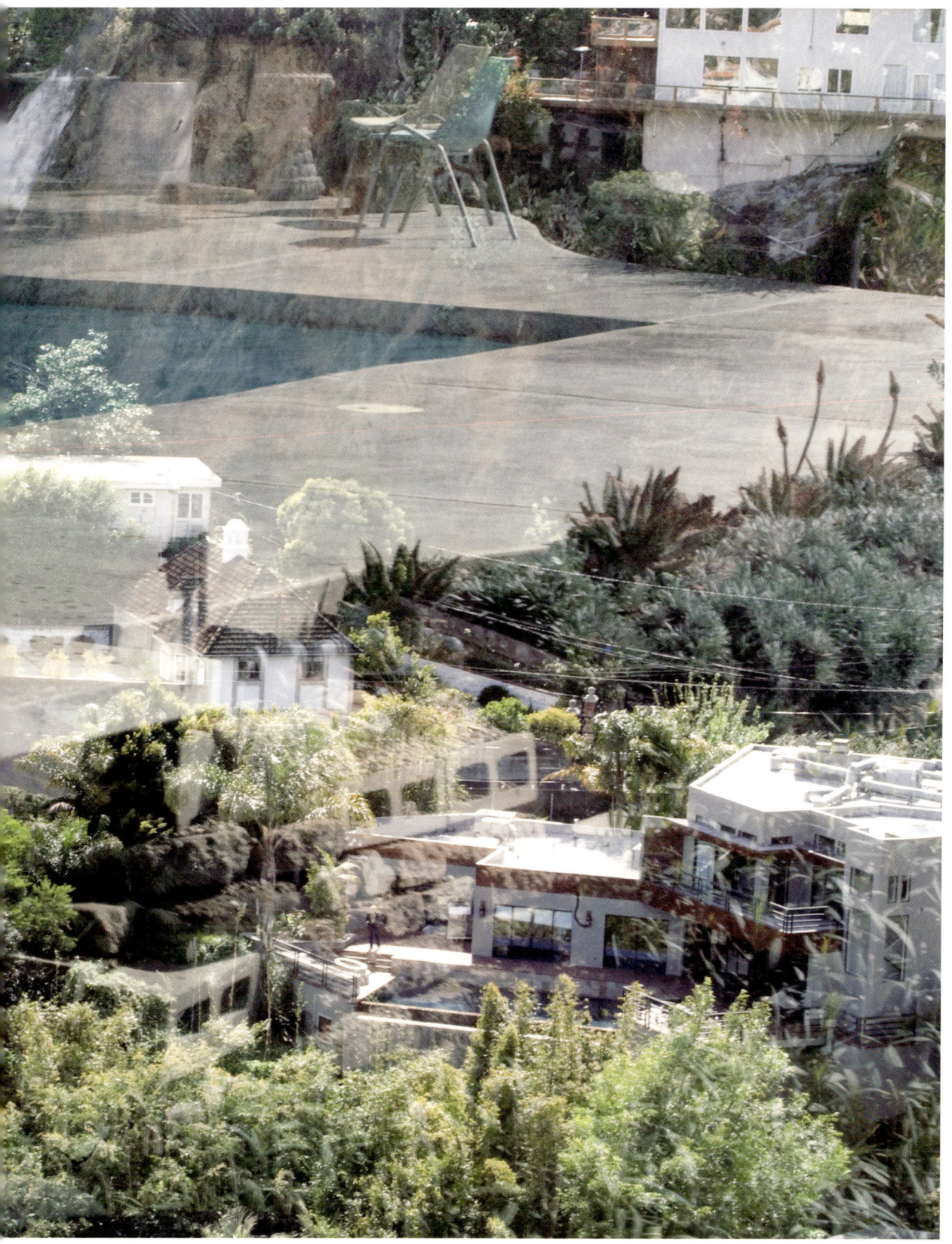

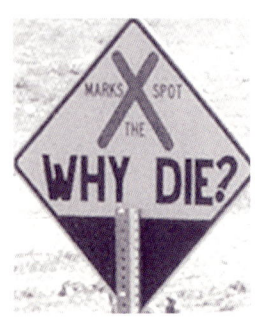

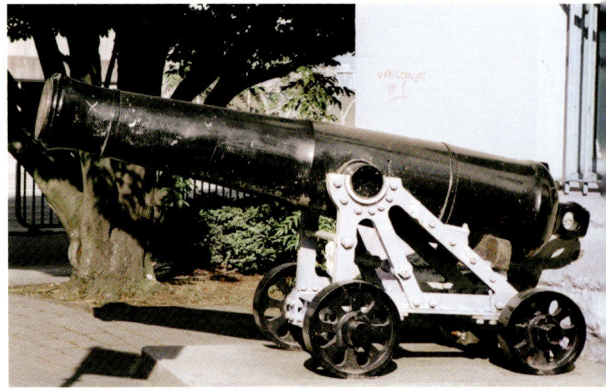

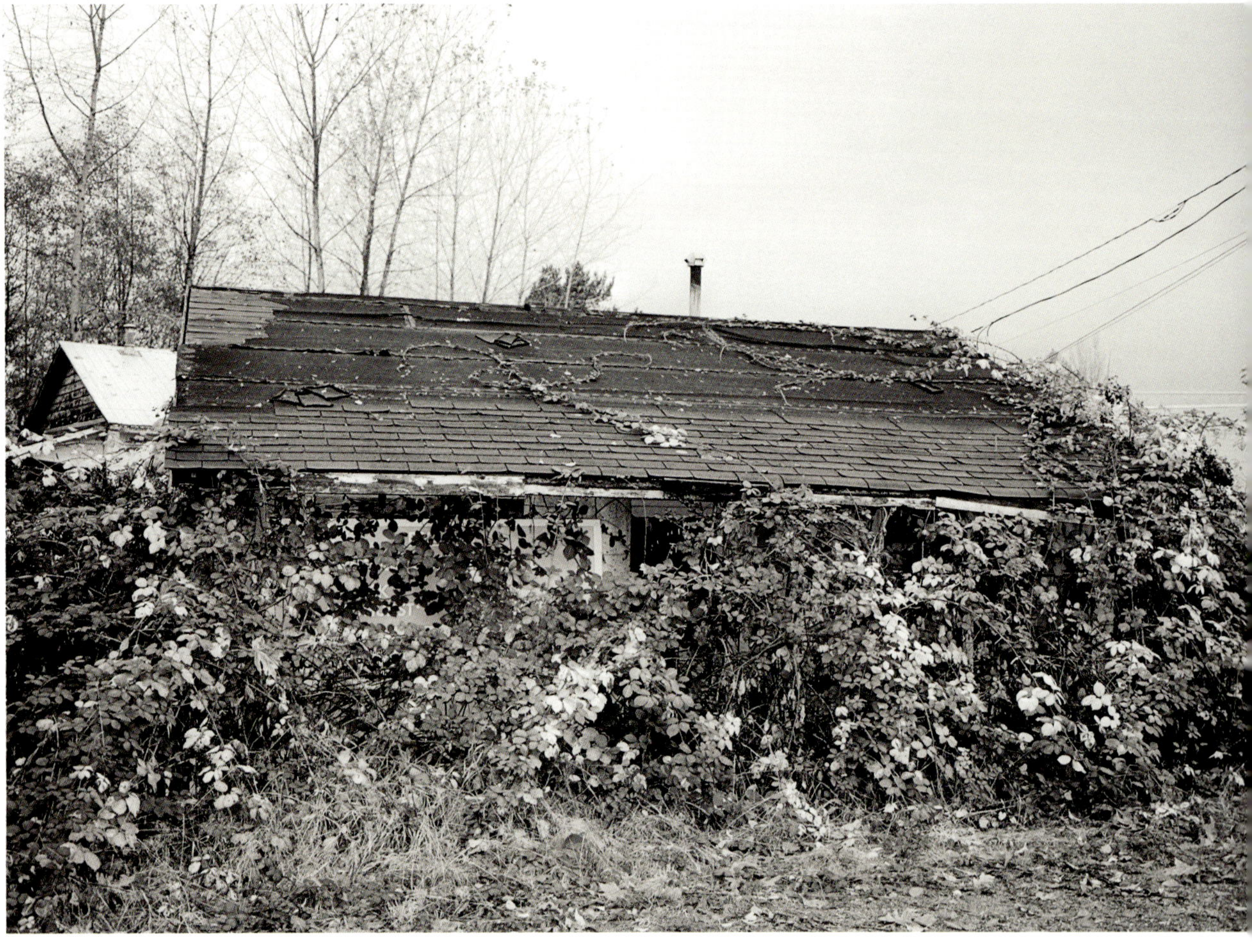

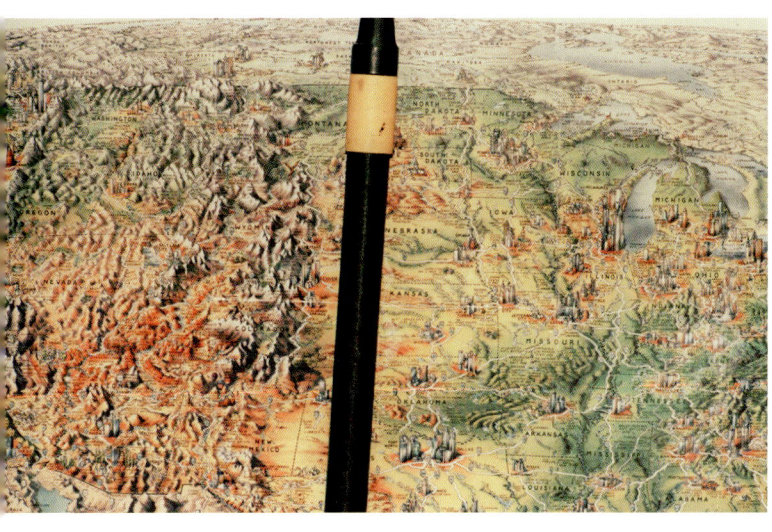

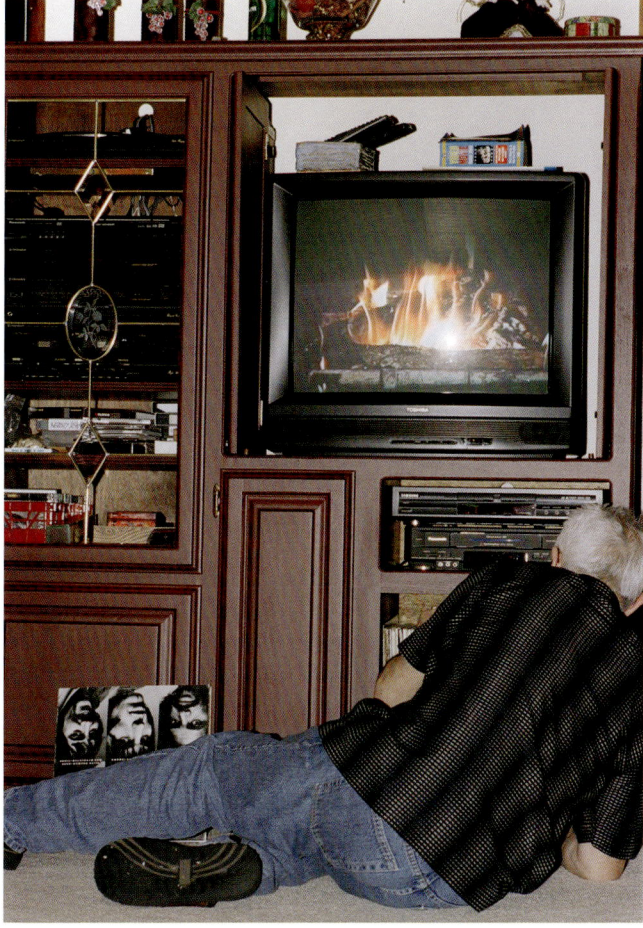

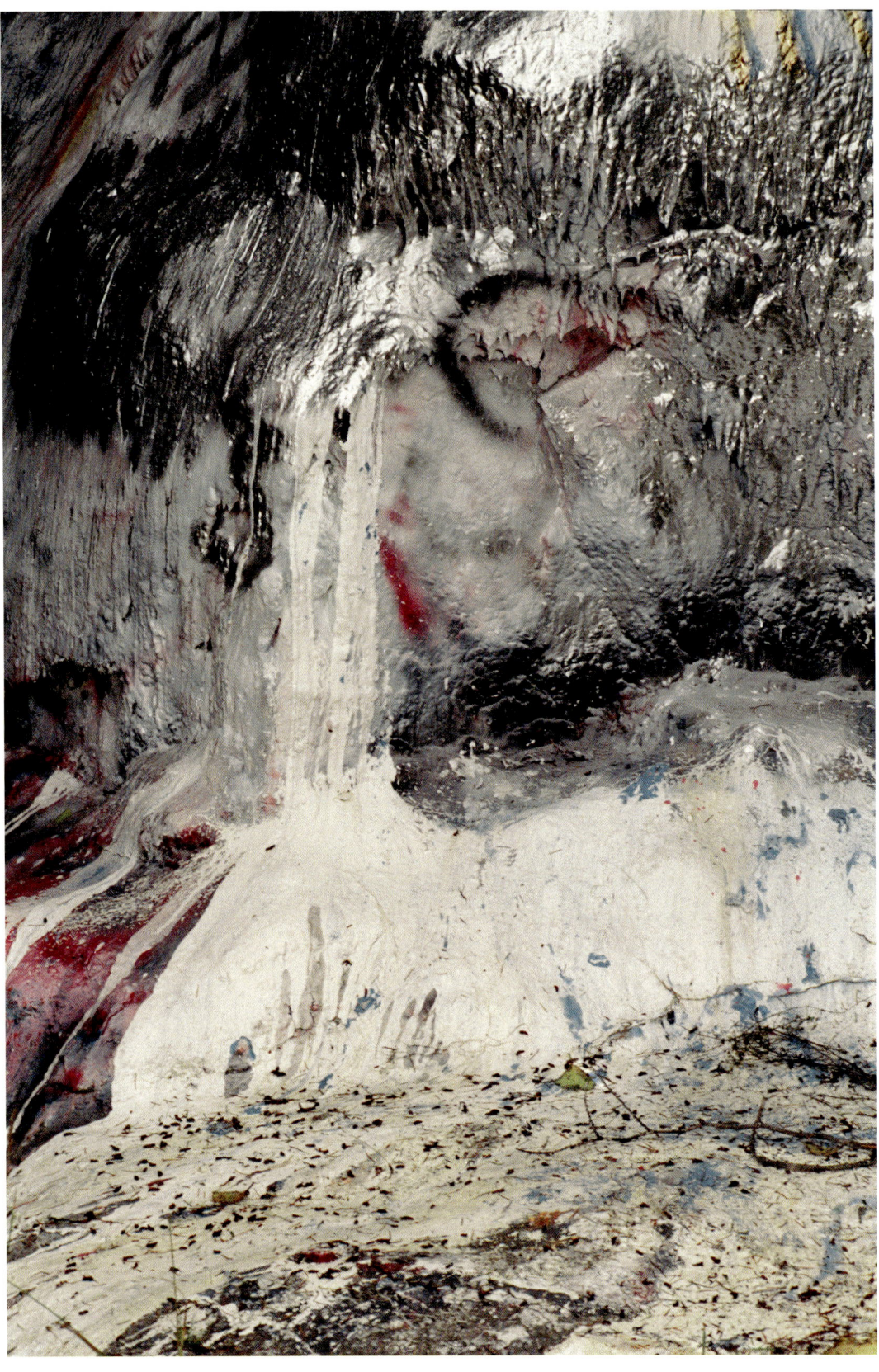

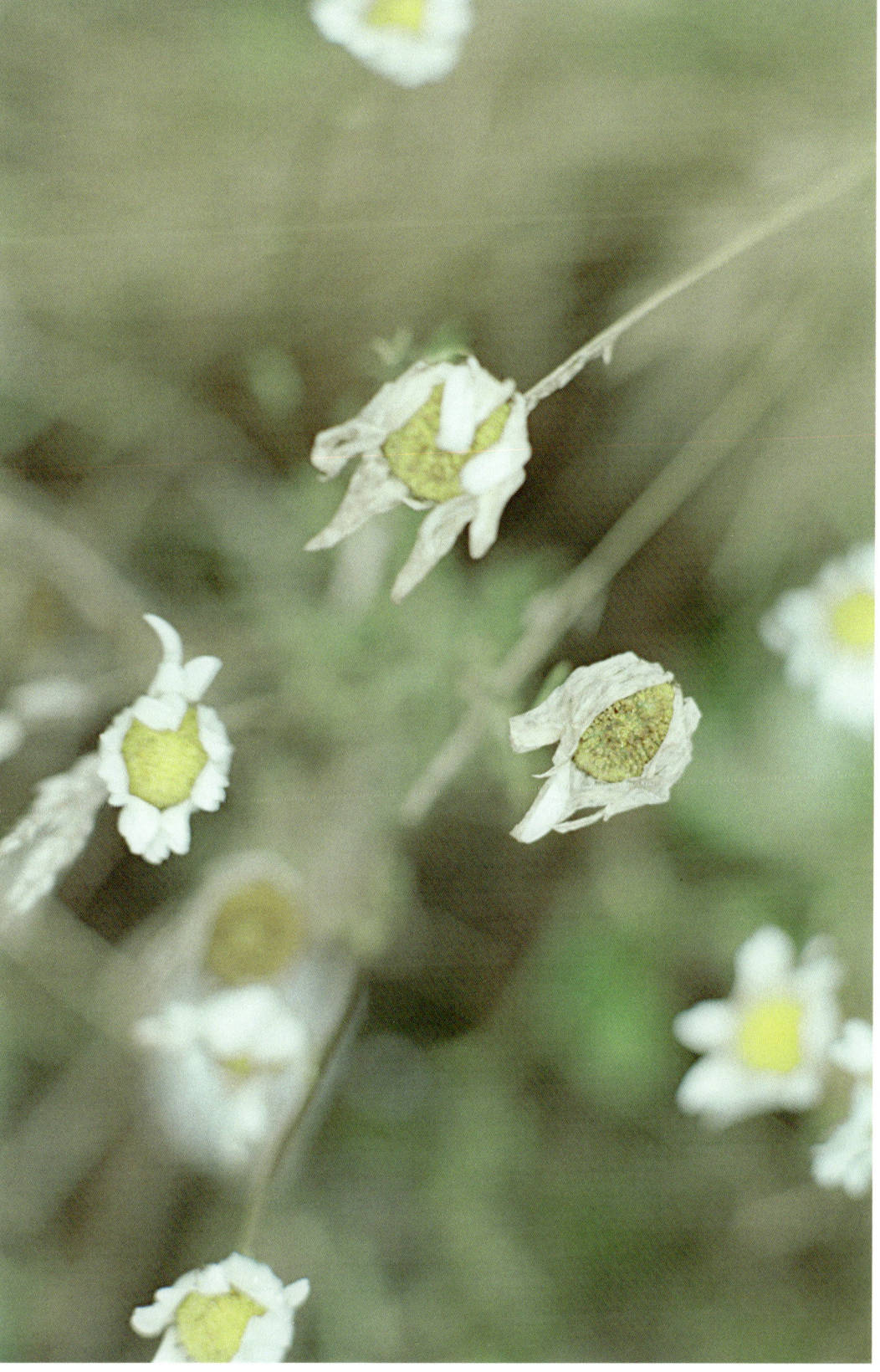

Mother Fucking Luke Cummo. Anyone who has put a ray of light in my blackened sky and the guy who invented breakdowns for inventing breakdowns, thank you for inventing breakdowns =)

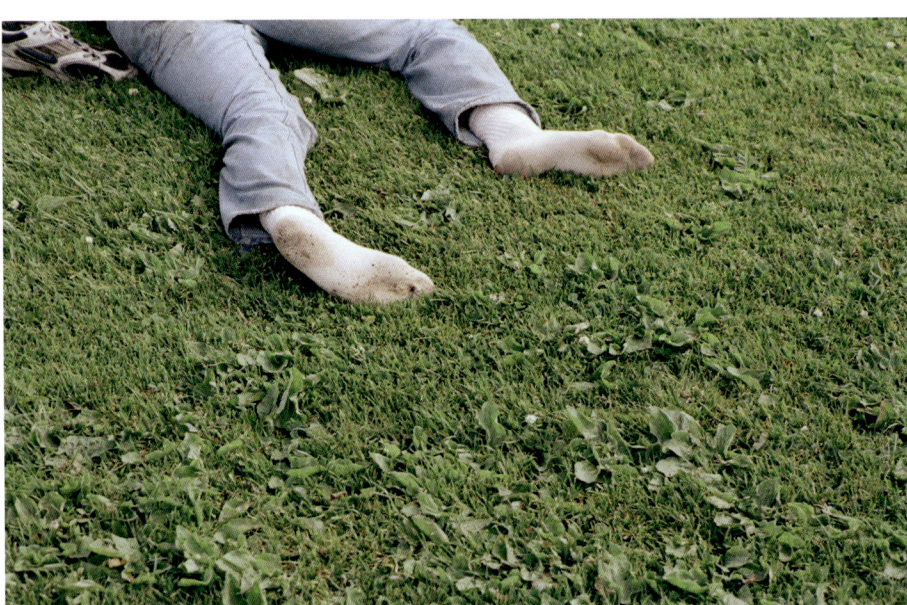

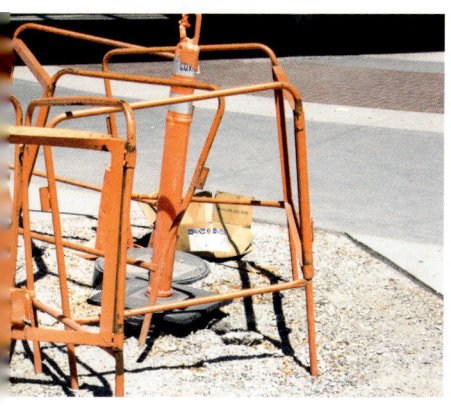

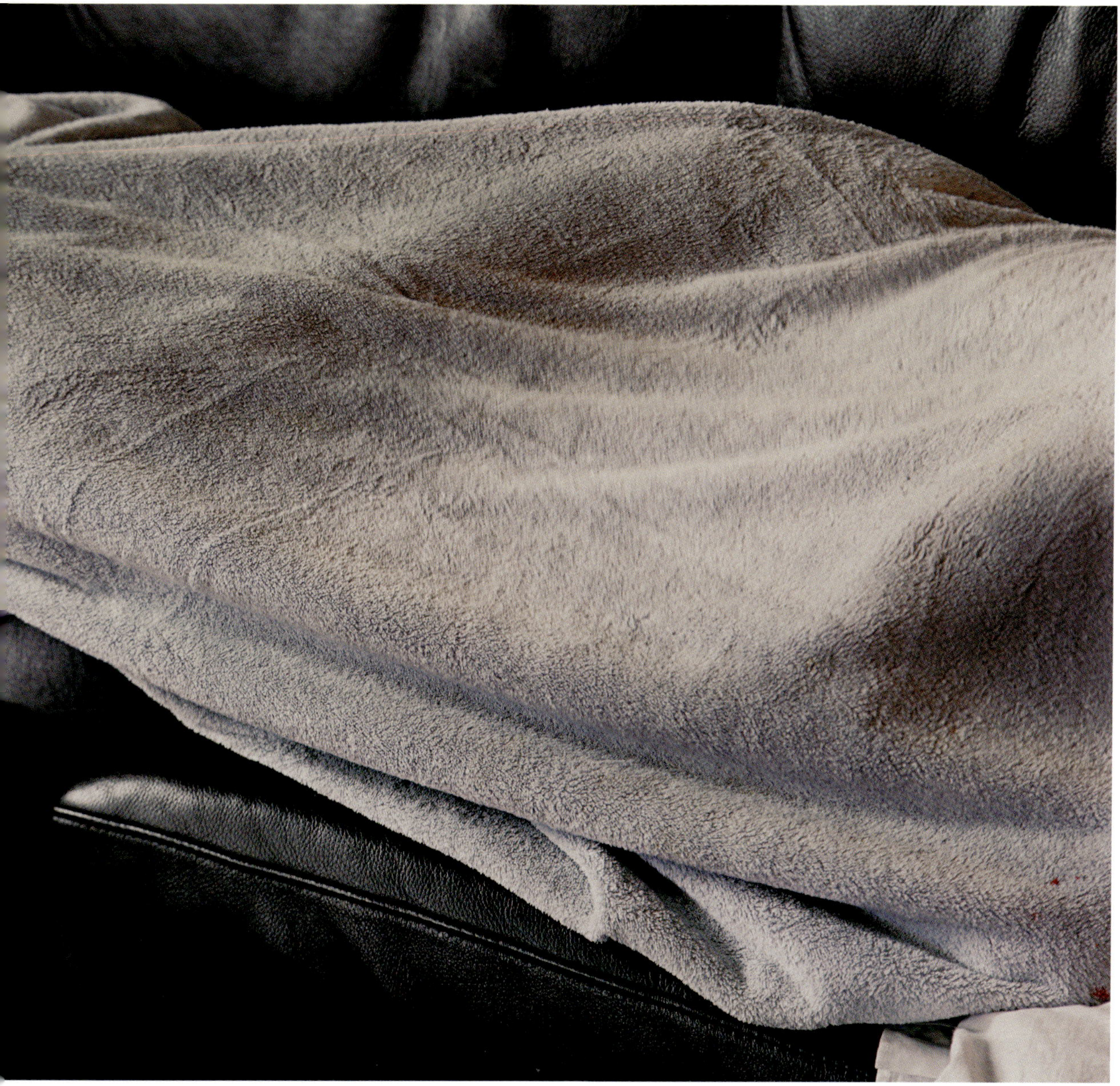

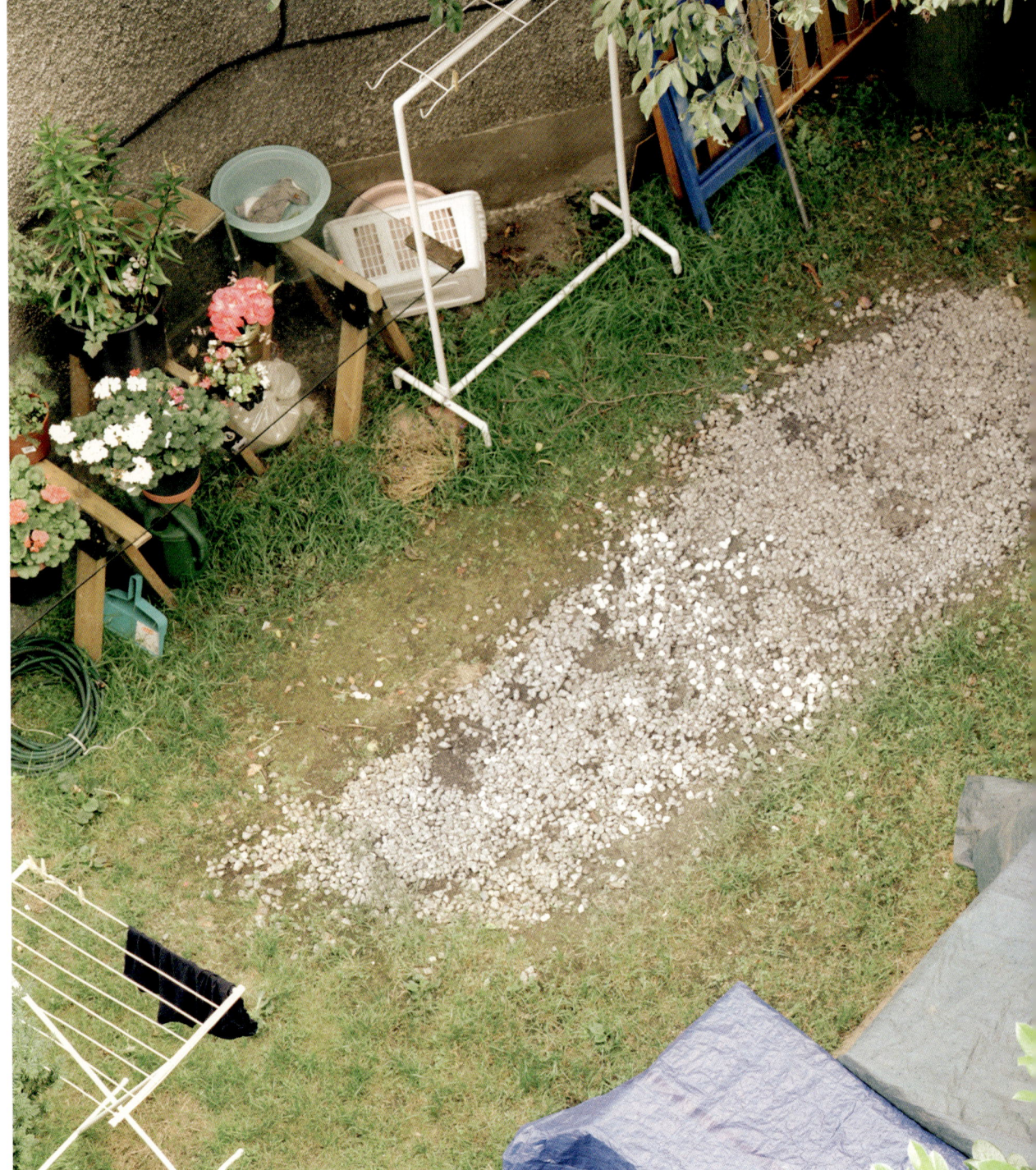

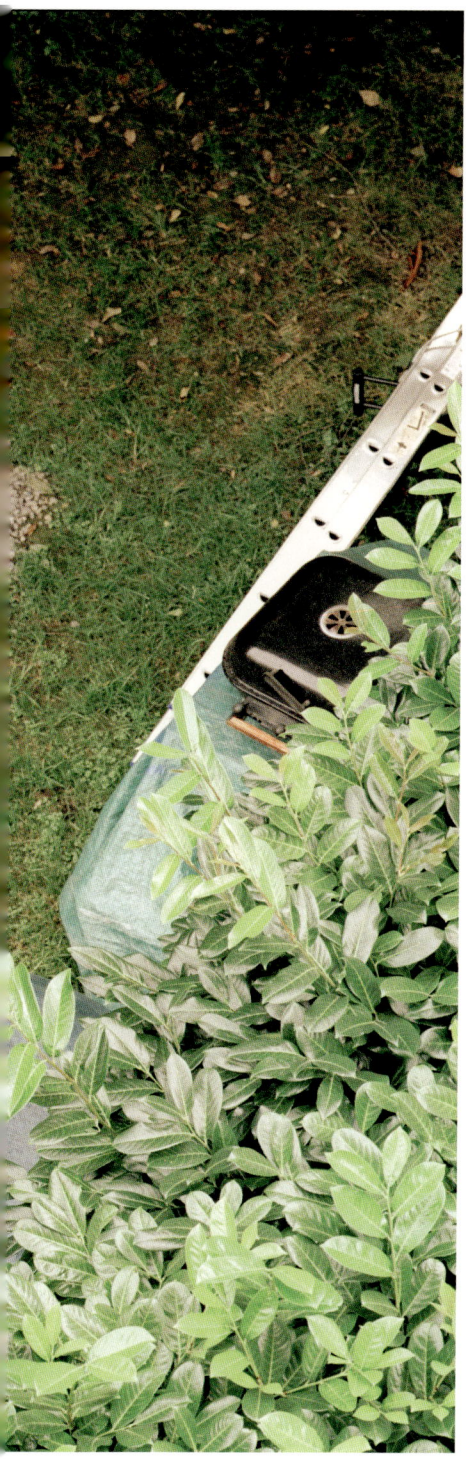

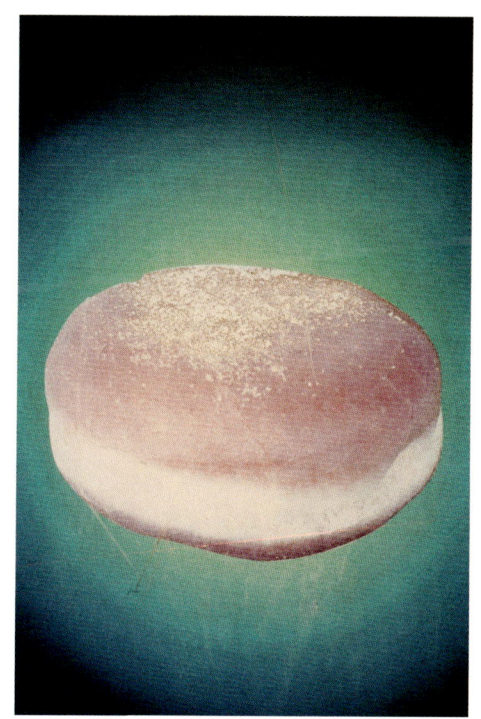

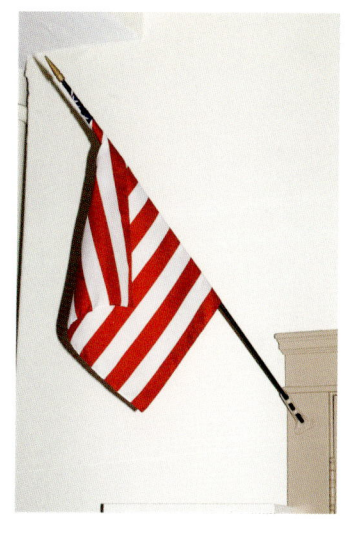

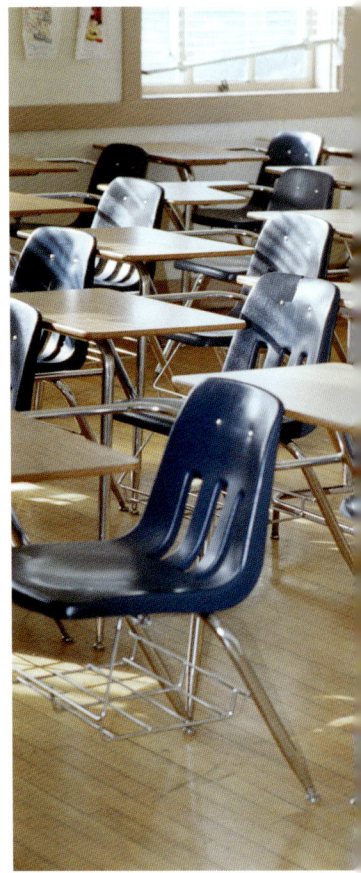

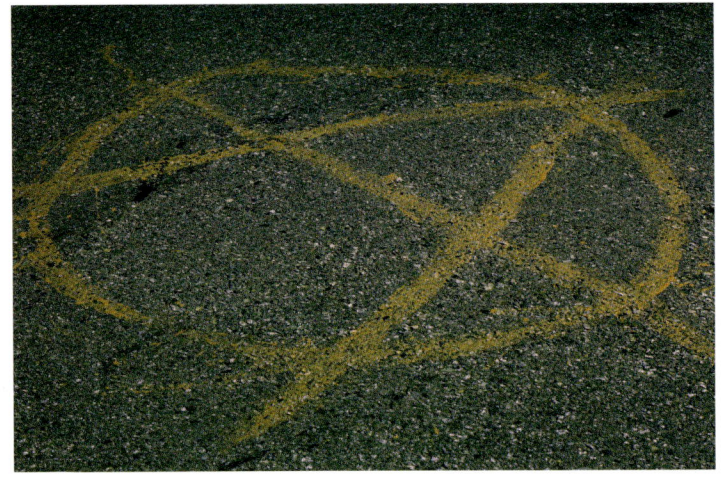

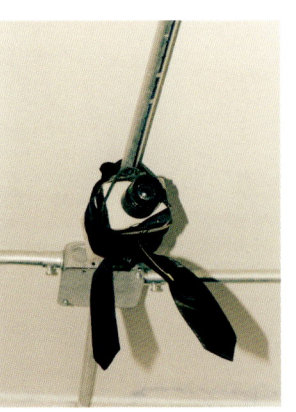

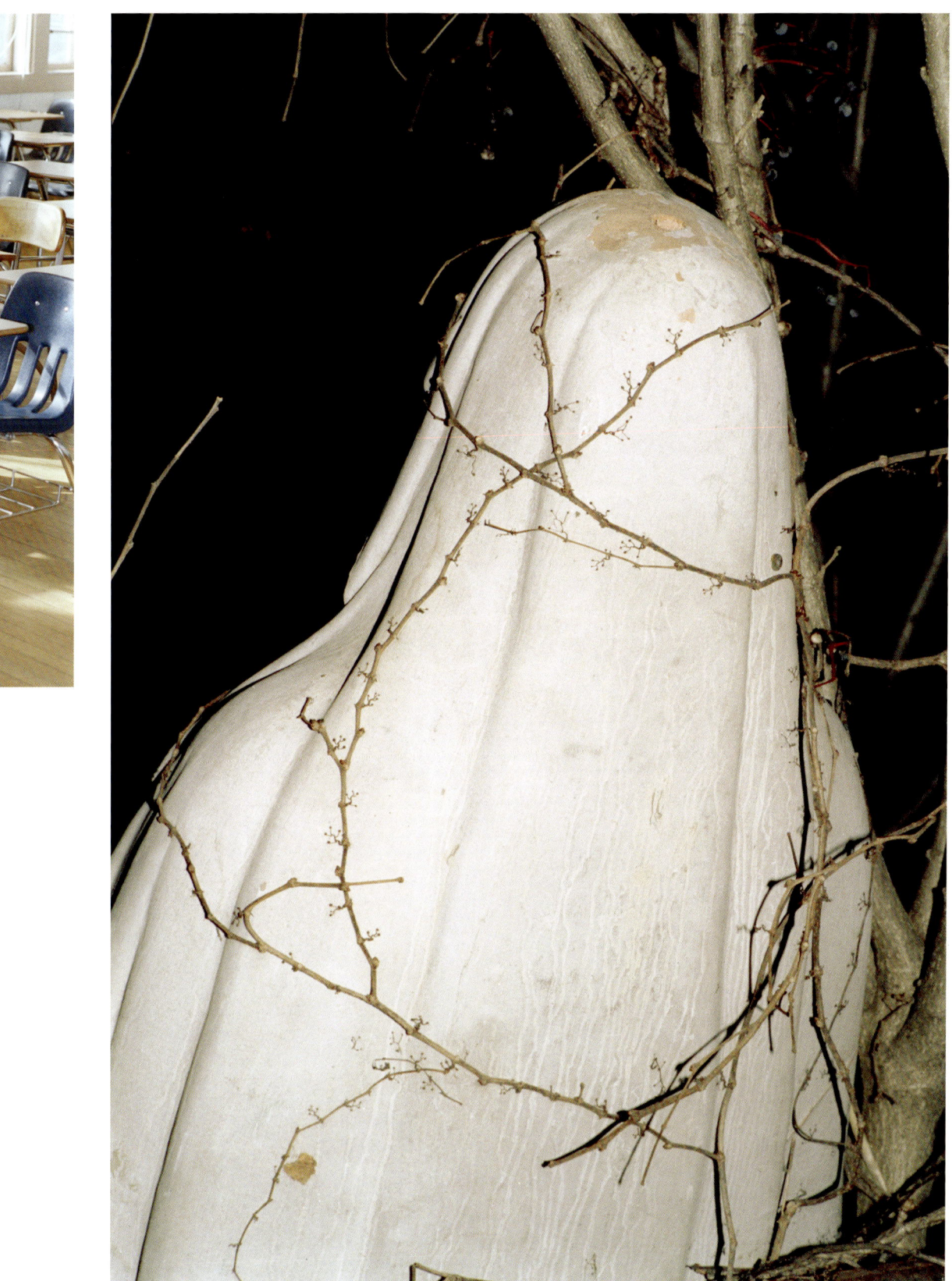

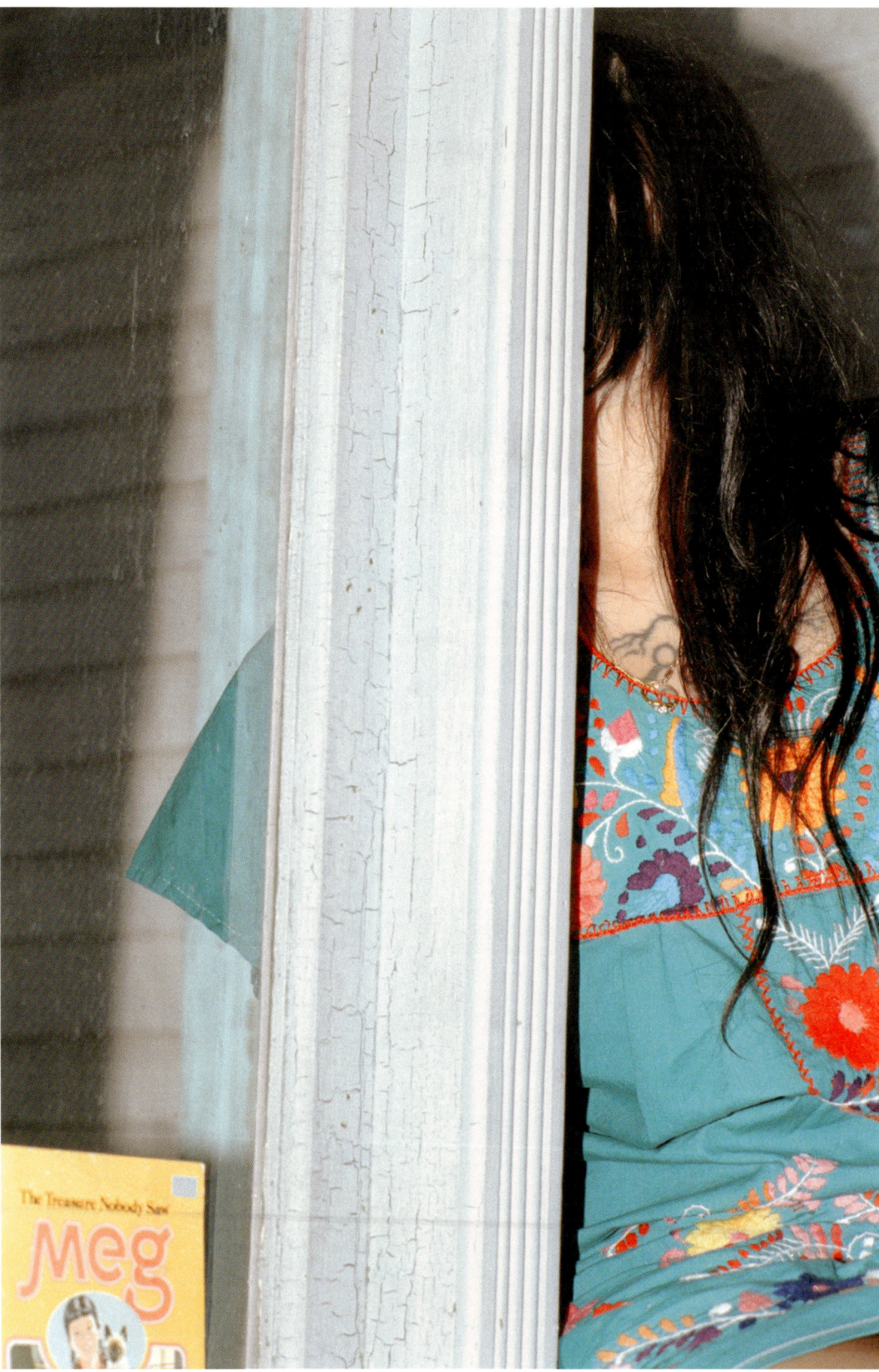

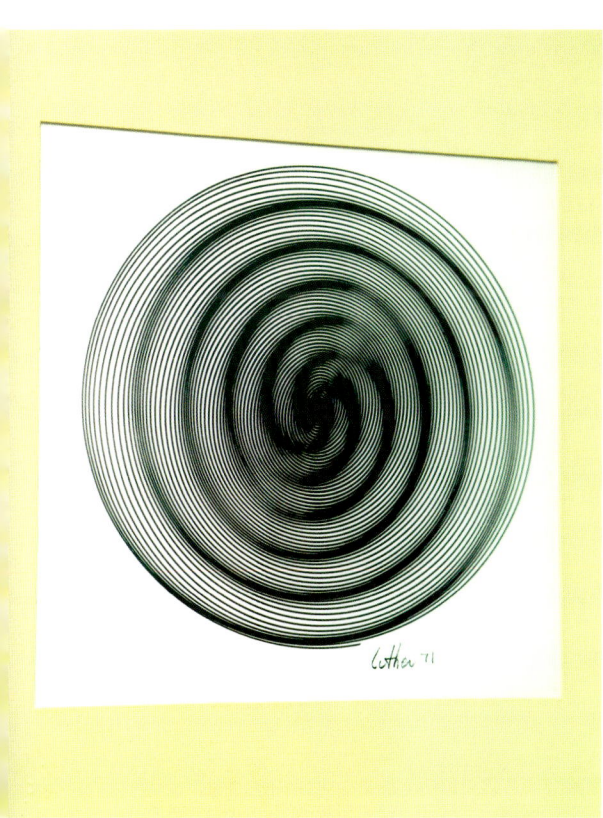

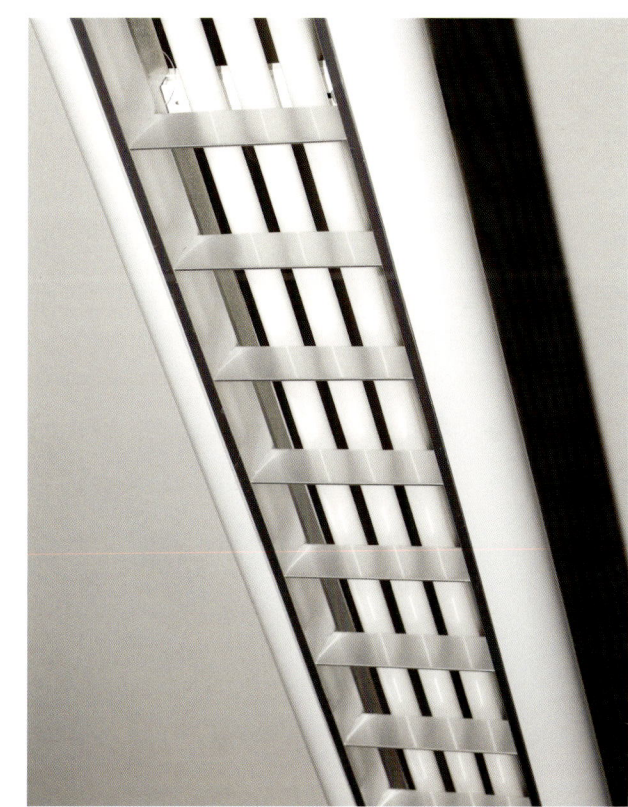

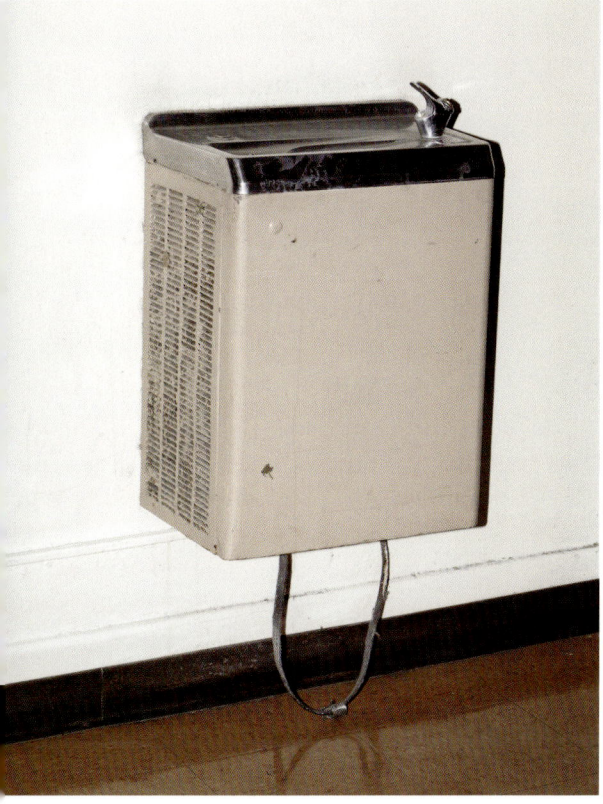

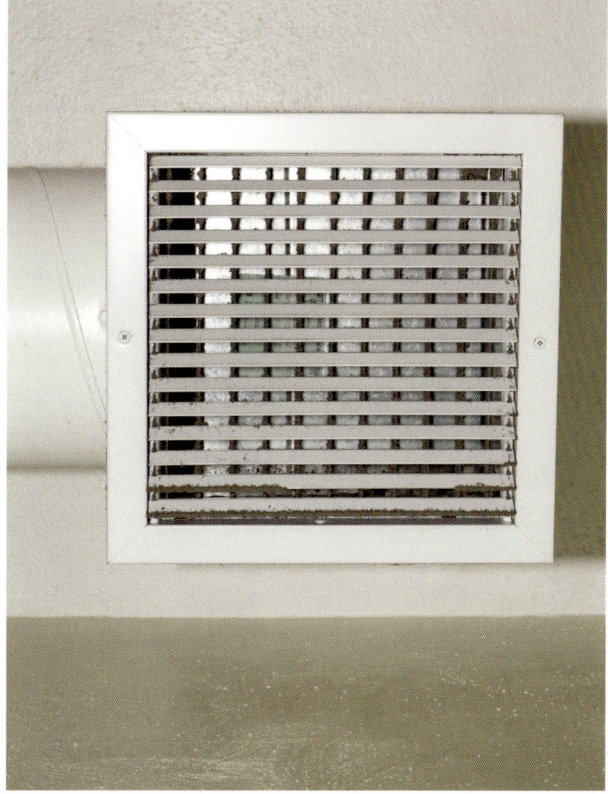

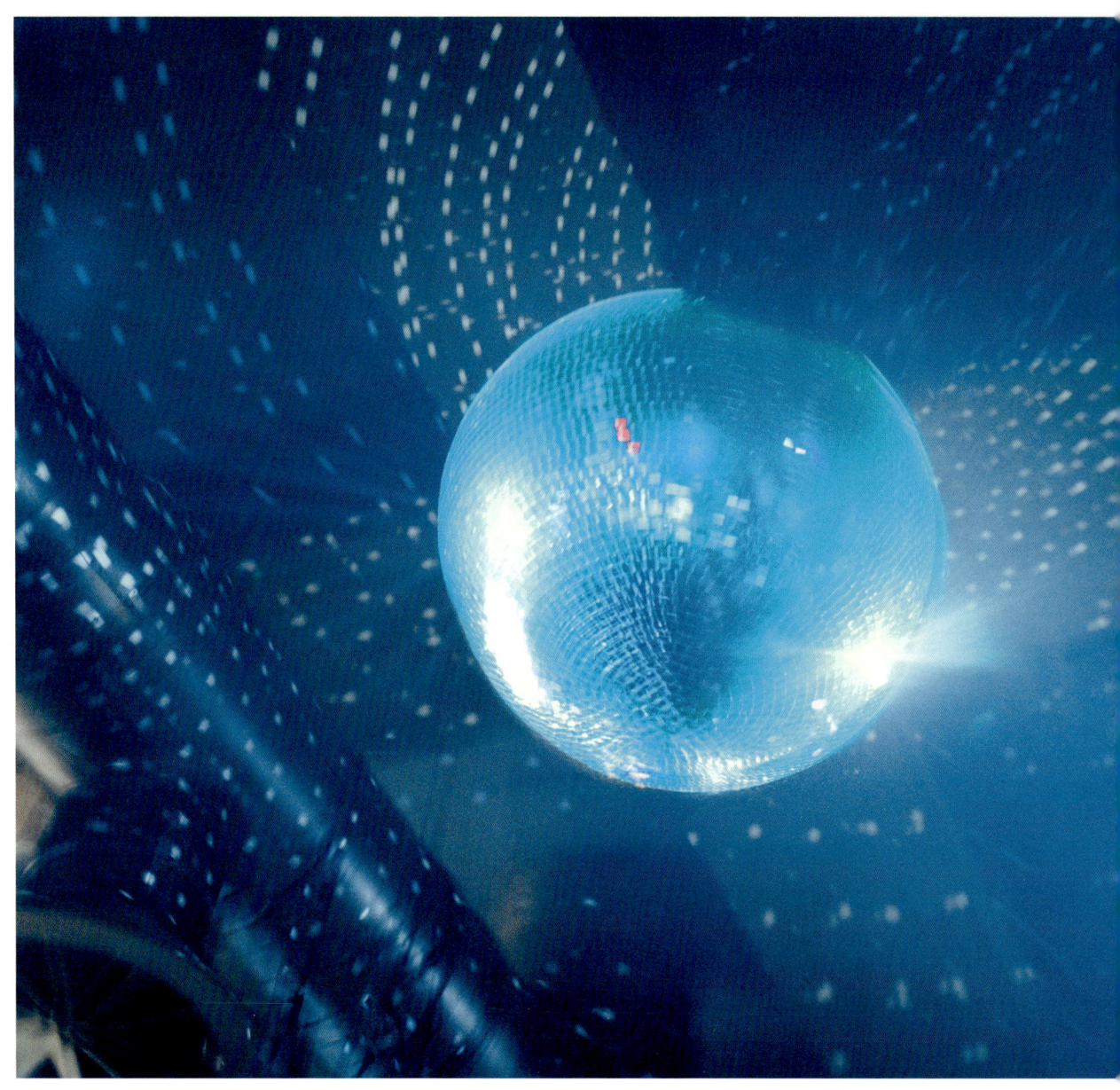

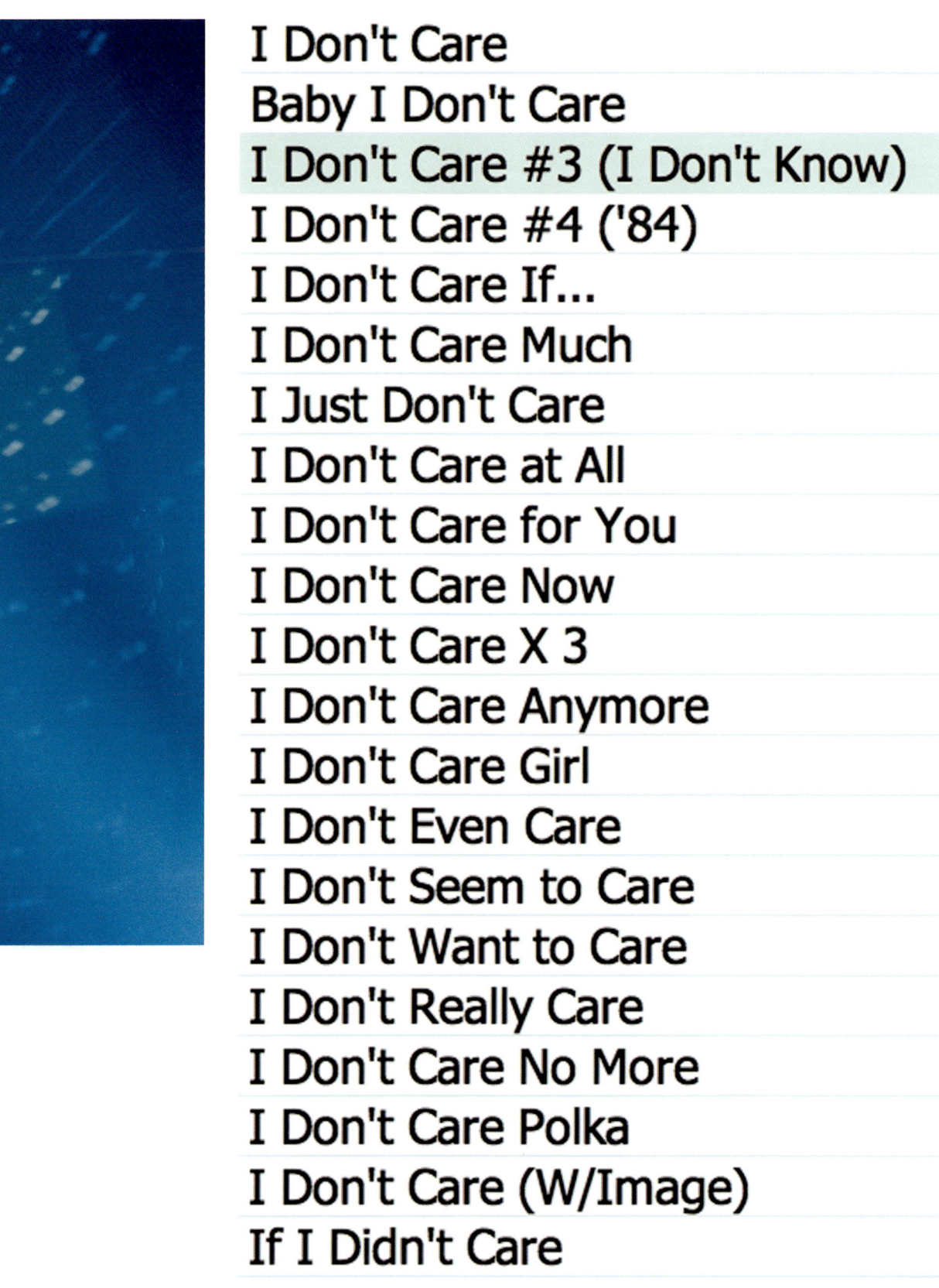

I Don't Care
Baby I Don't Care
I Don't Care #3 (I Don't Know)
I Don't Care #4 ('84)
I Don't Care If...
I Don't Care Much
I Just Don't Care
I Don't Care at All
I Don't Care for You
I Don't Care Now
I Don't Care X 3
I Don't Care Anymore
I Don't Care Girl
I Don't Even Care
I Don't Seem to Care
I Don't Want to Care
I Don't Really Care
I Don't Care No More
I Don't Care Polka
I Don't Care (W/Image)
If I Didn't Care

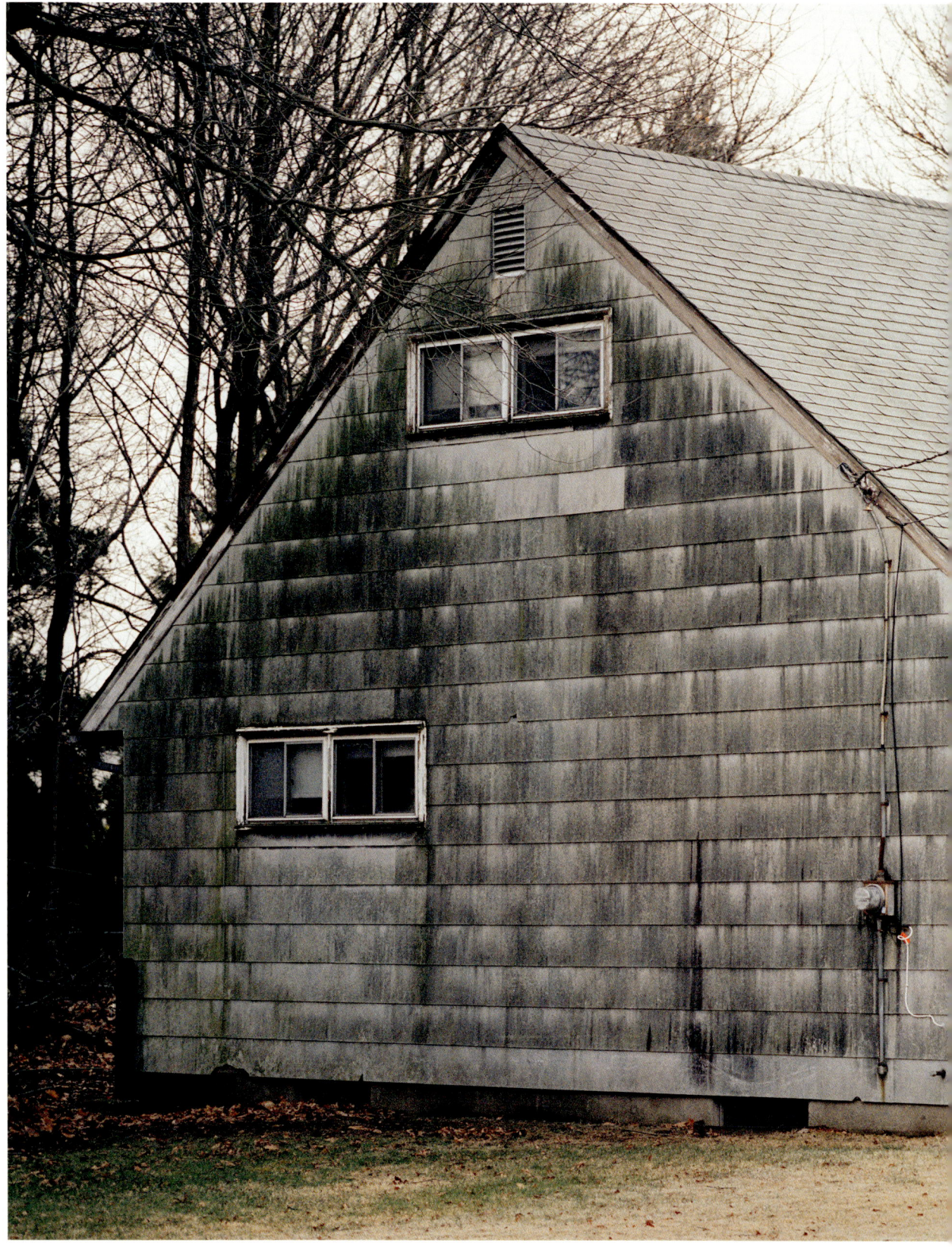

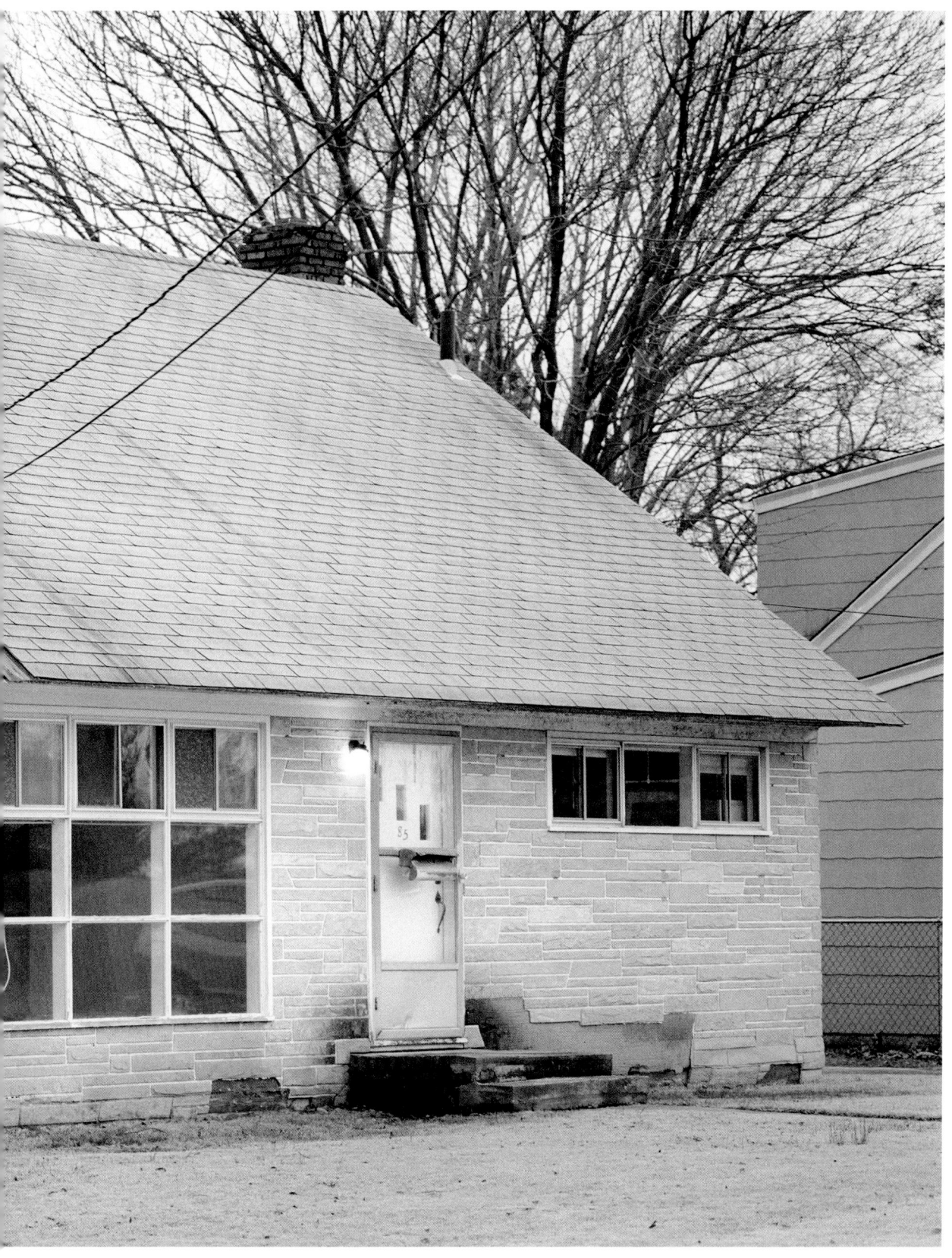

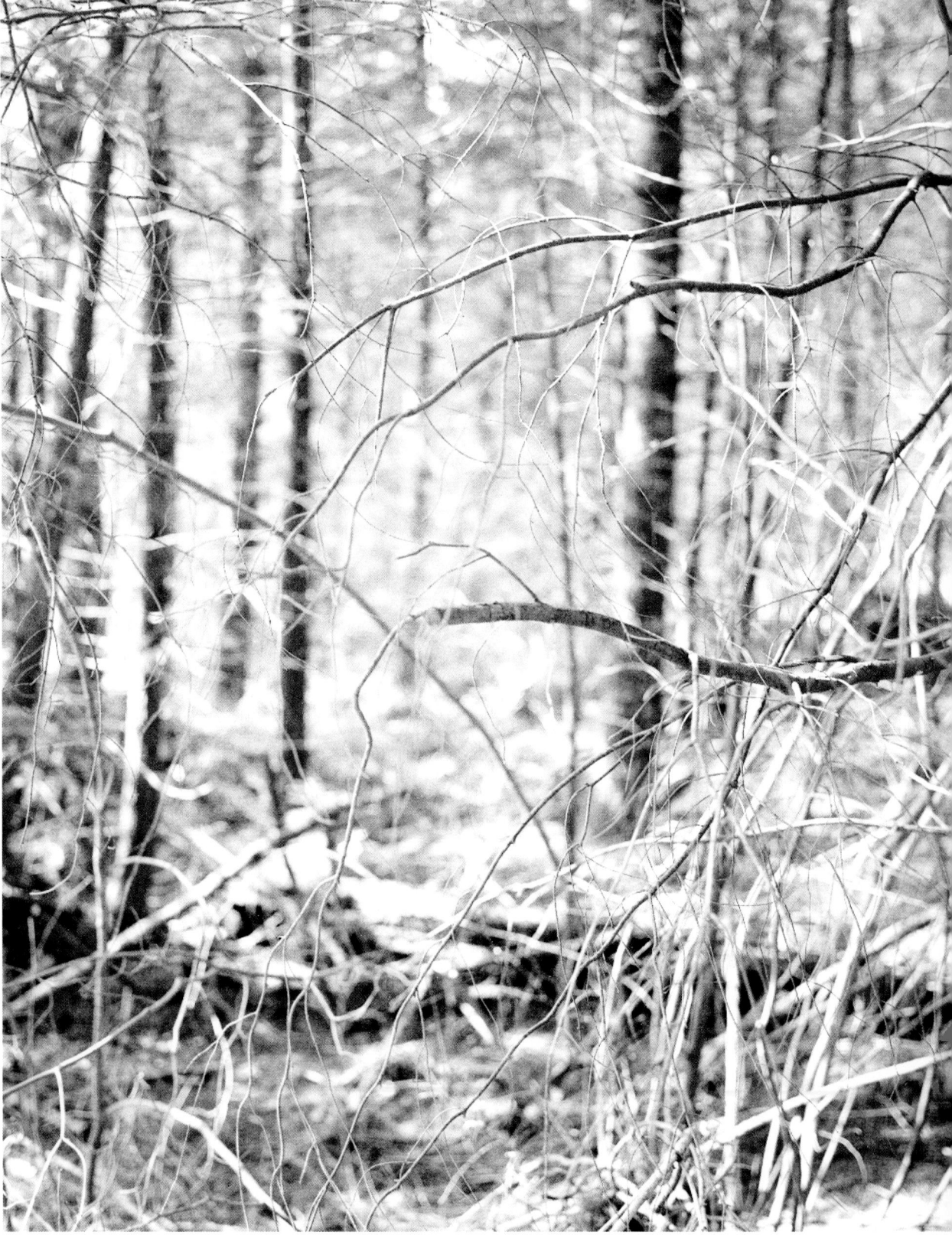

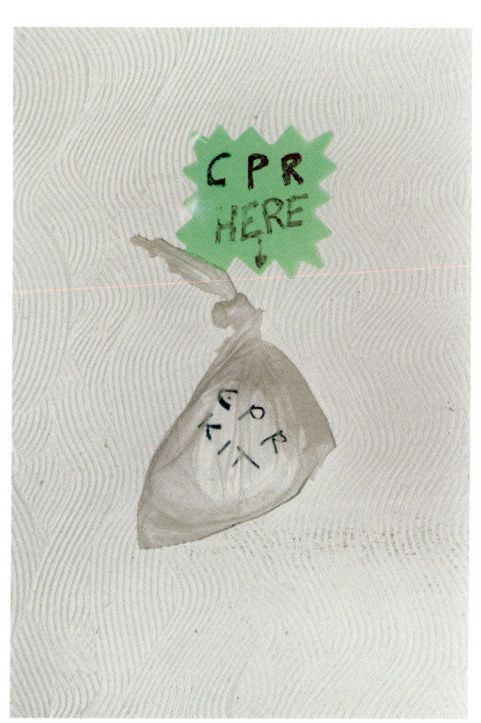

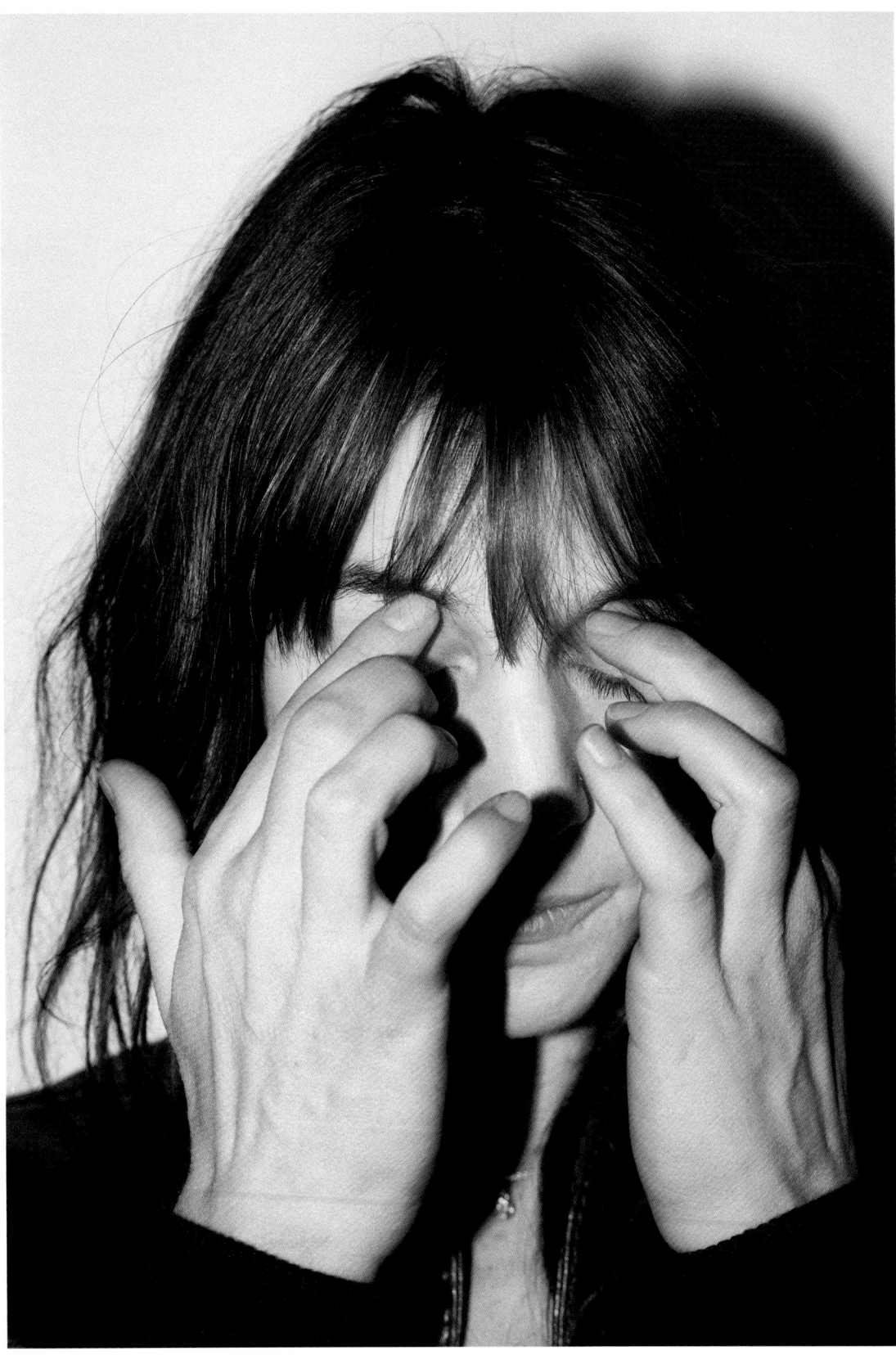

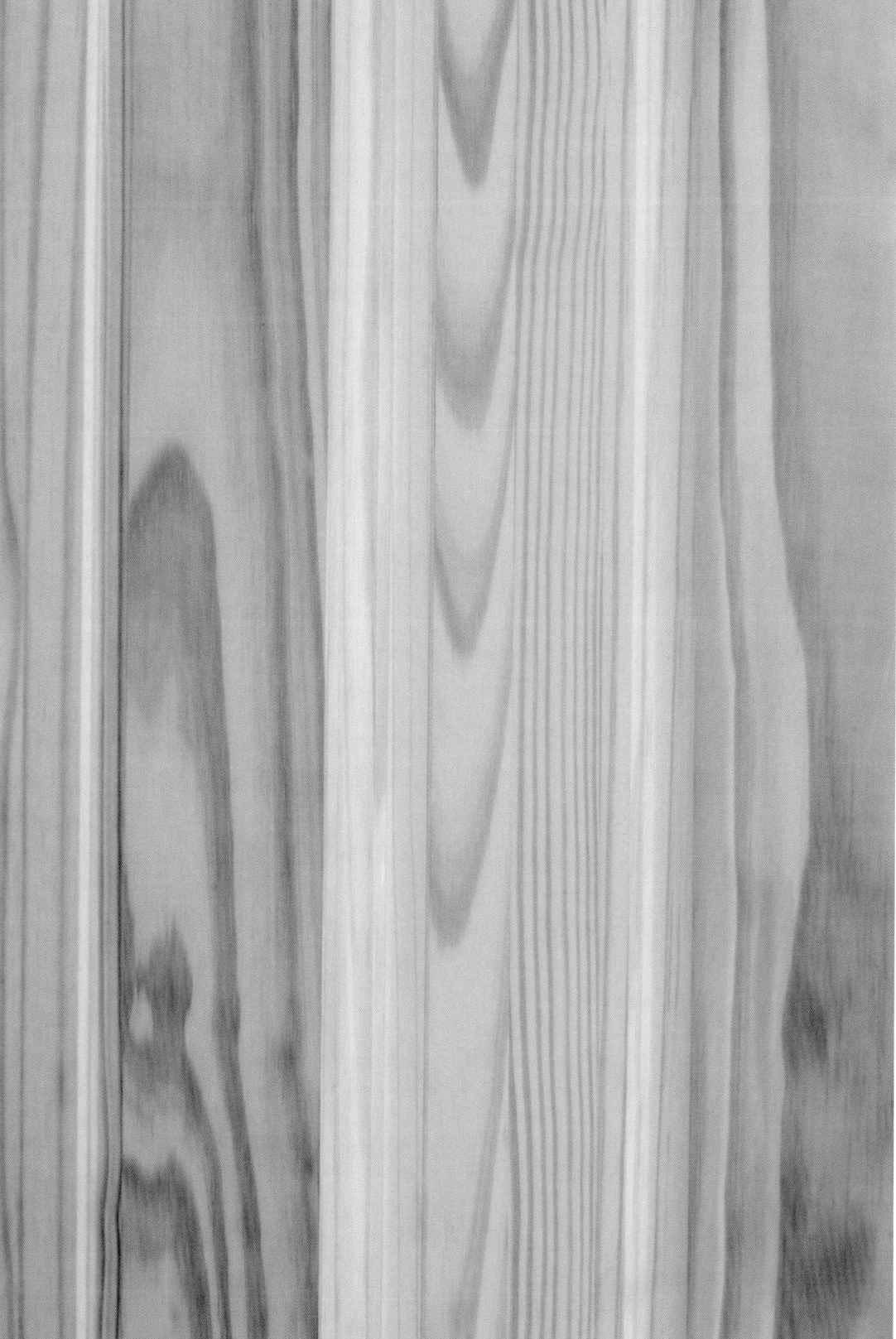

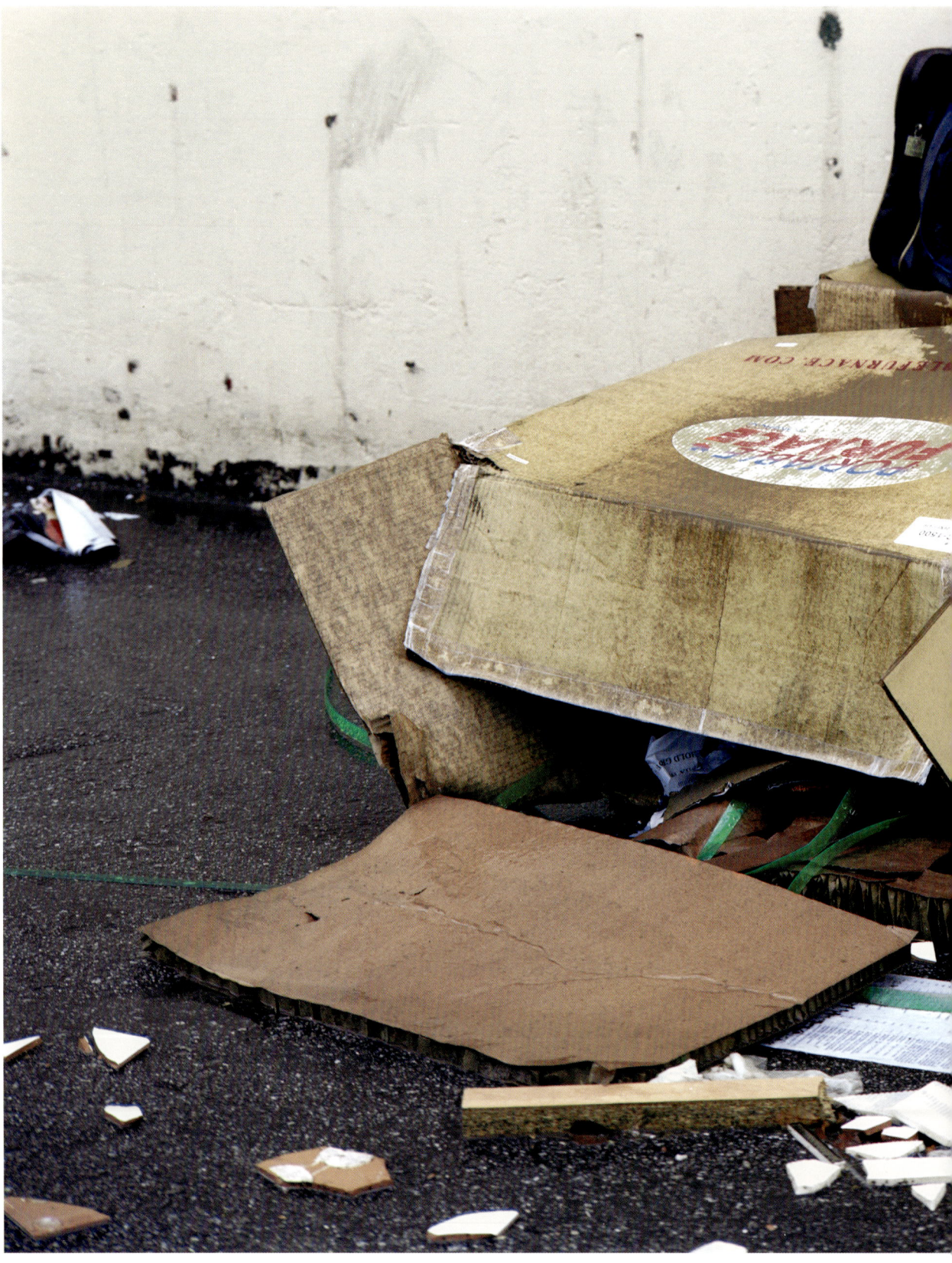

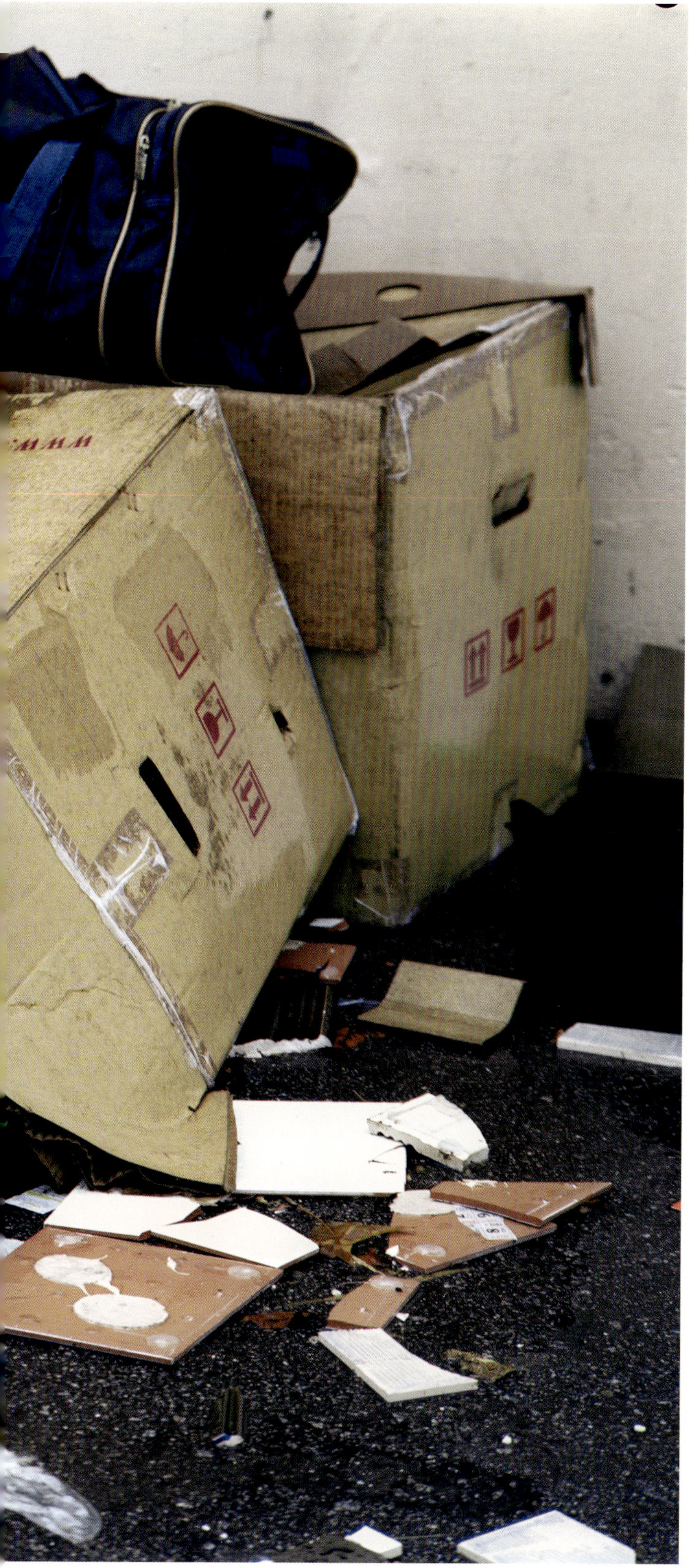

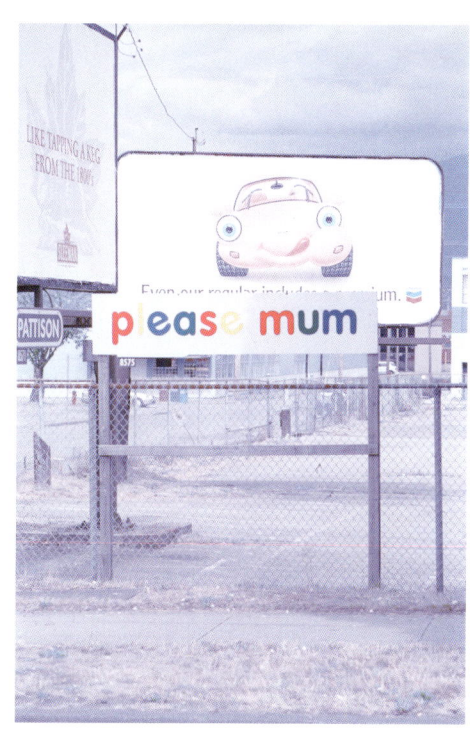

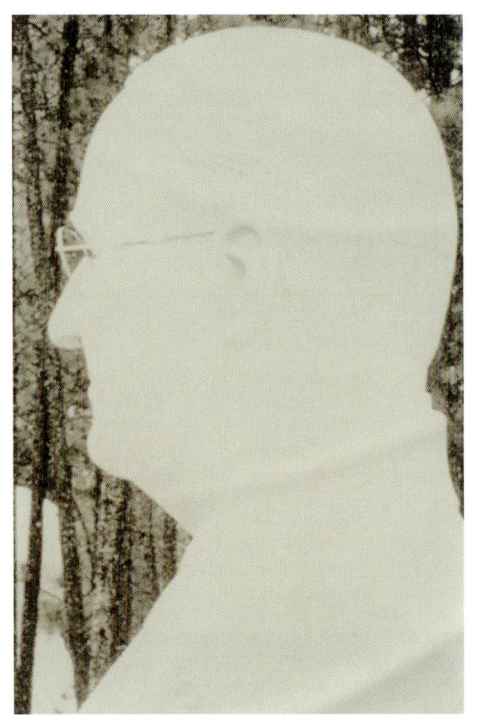
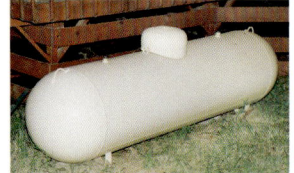
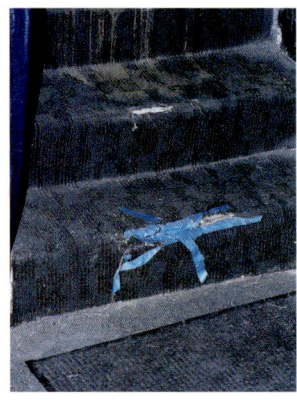
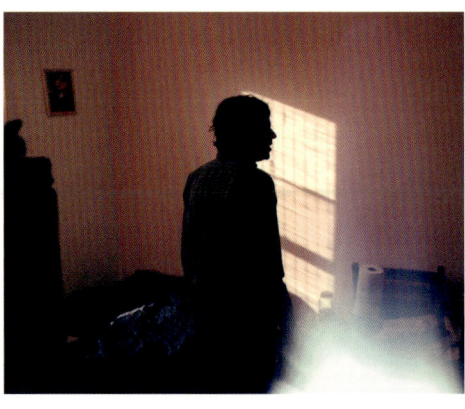

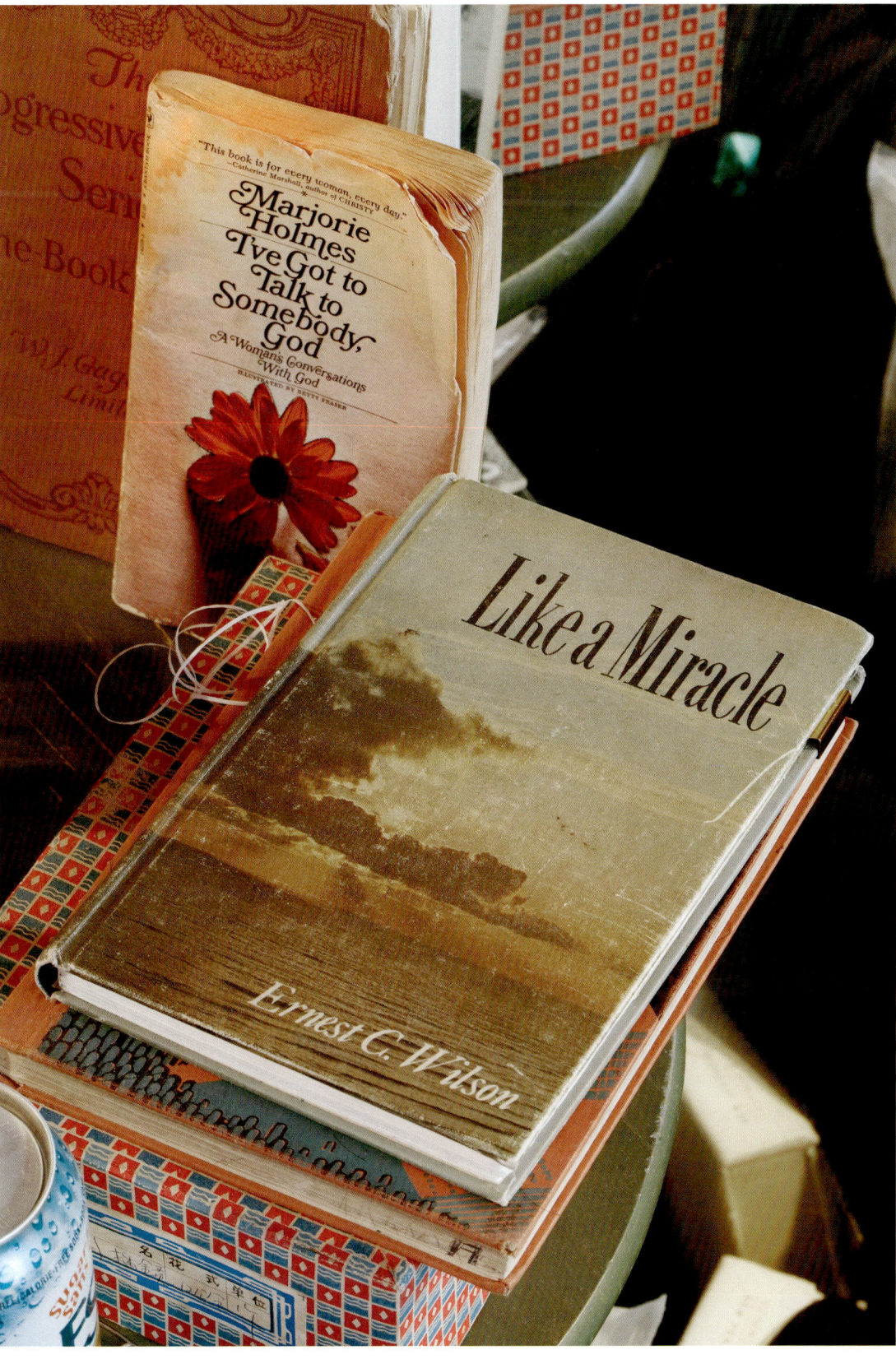

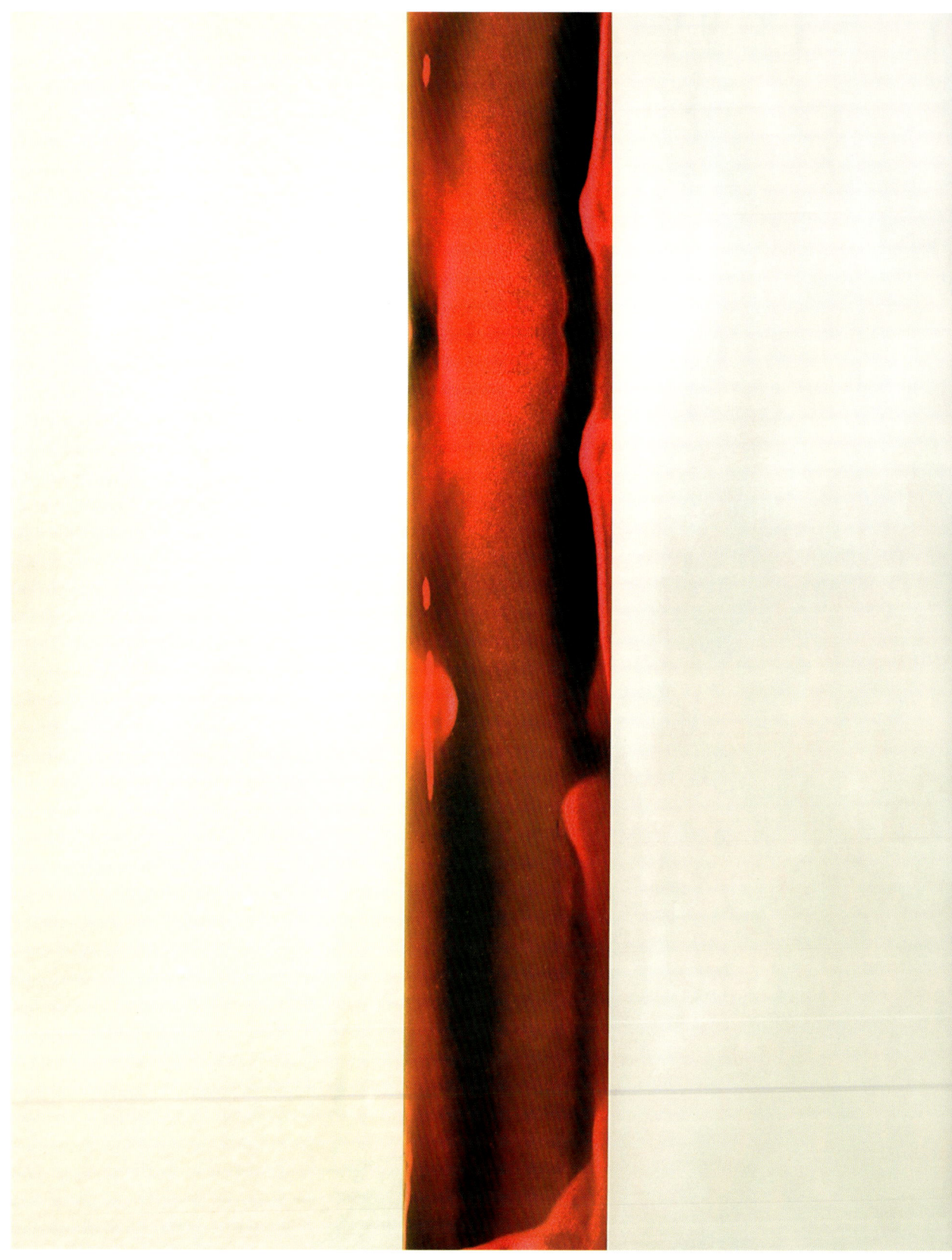

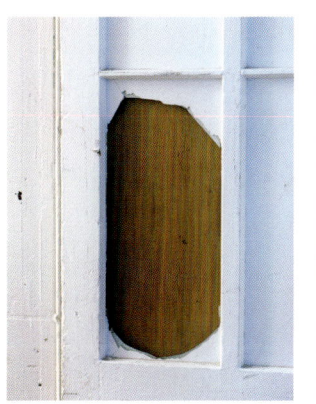 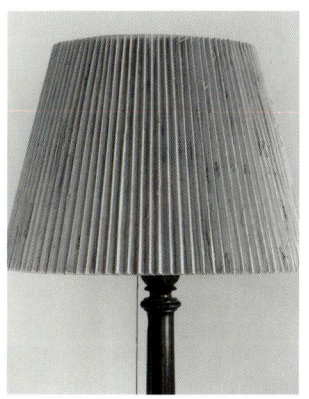 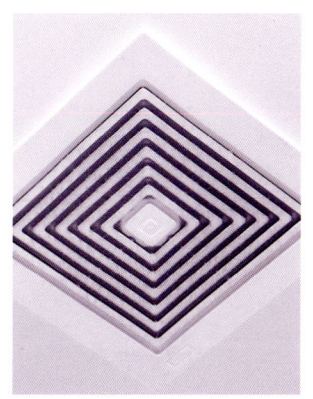

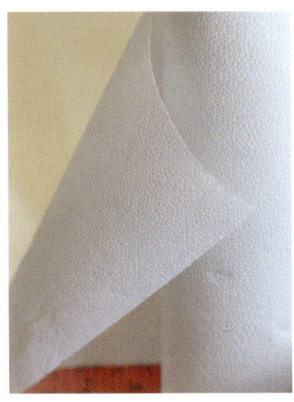
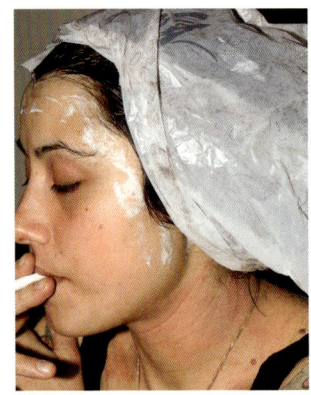
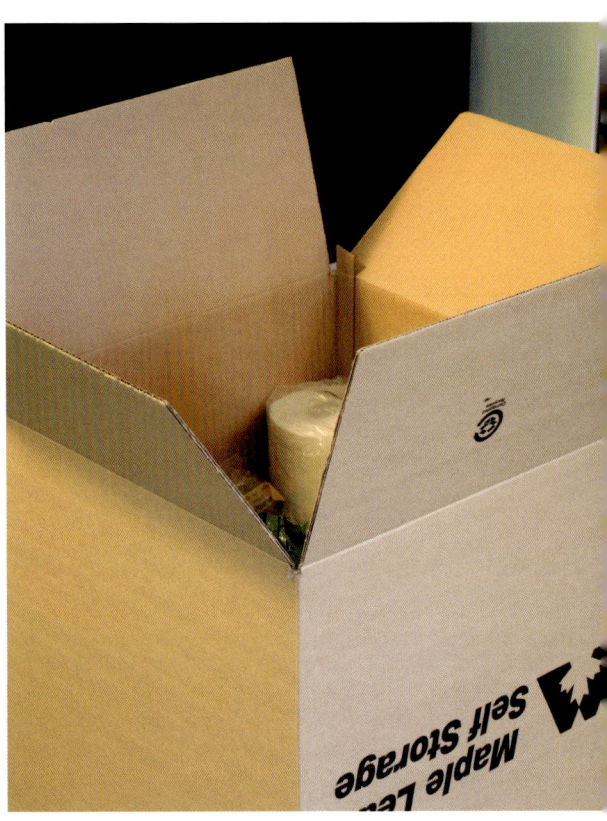
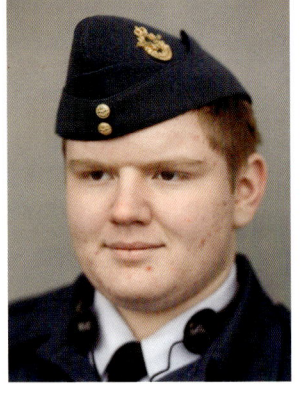
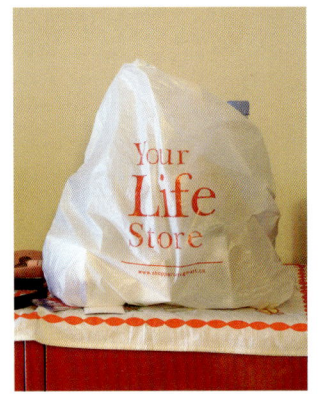
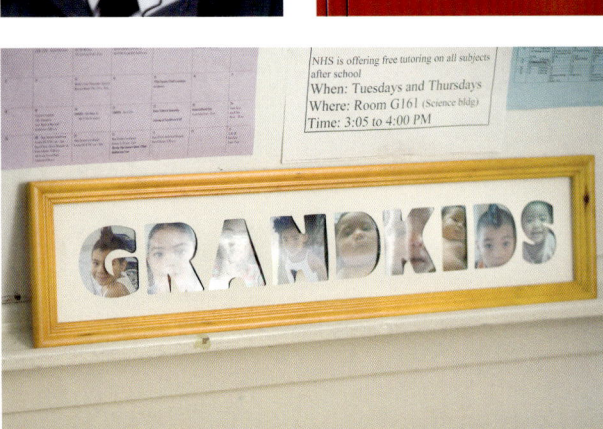

NHS is offering free tutoring on all subjects after school
When: Tuesdays and Thursdays
Where: Room G161 (Science bldg)
Time: 3:05 to 4:00 PM

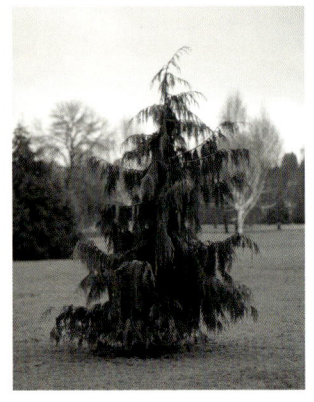
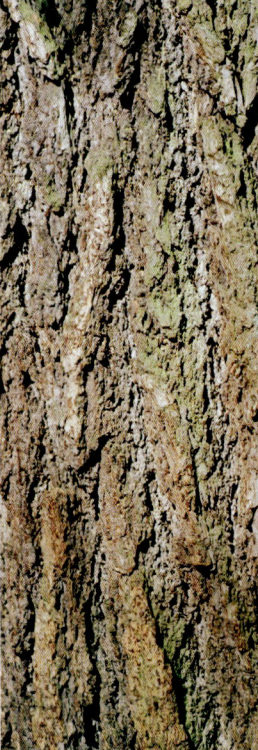
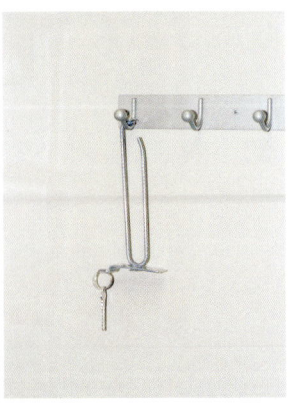
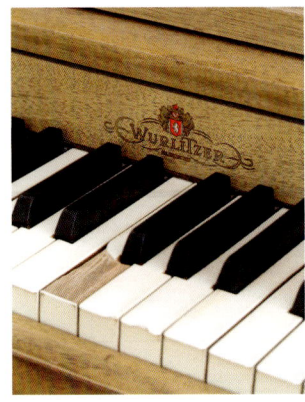
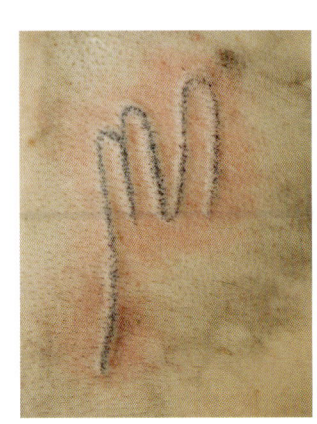

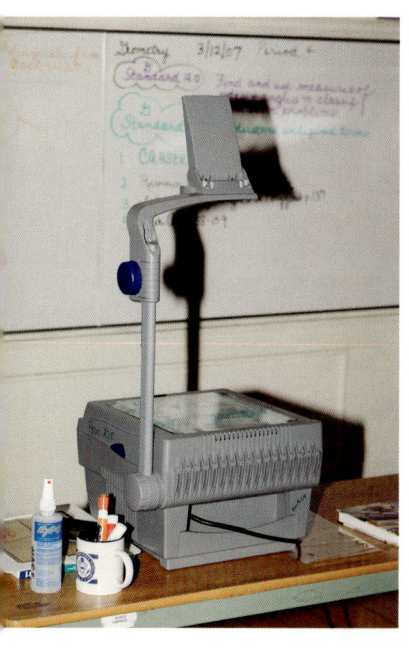

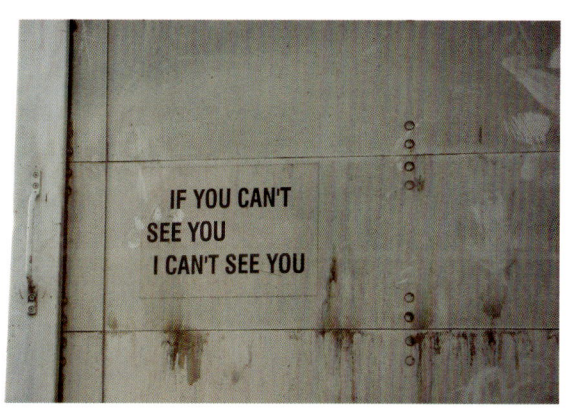

IF YOU CAN'T
SEE YOU
I CAN'T SEE YOU

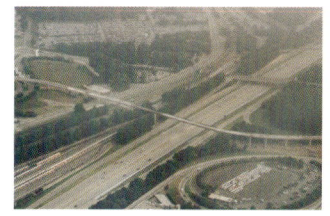

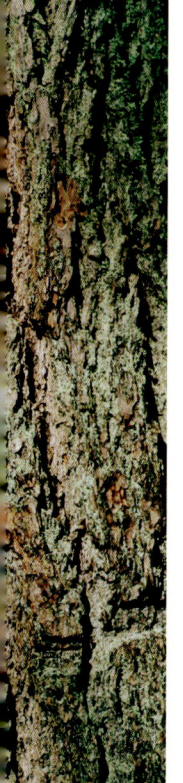

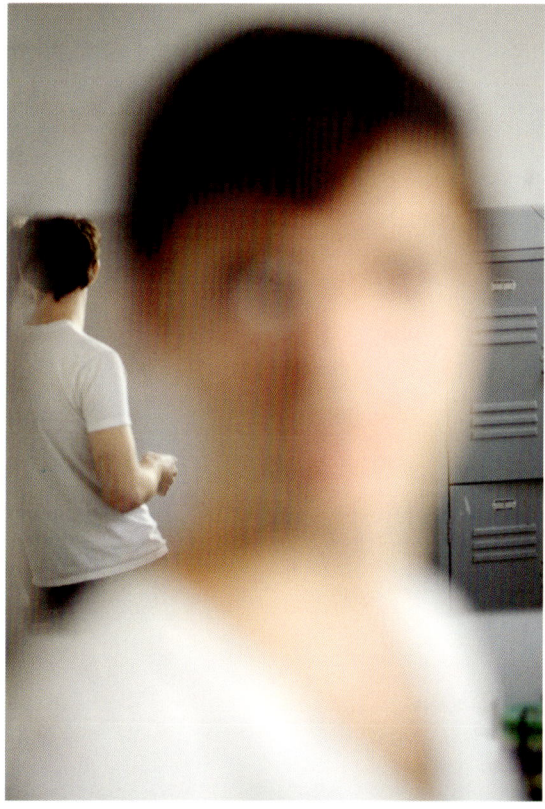

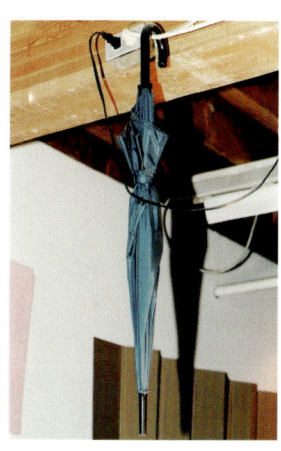

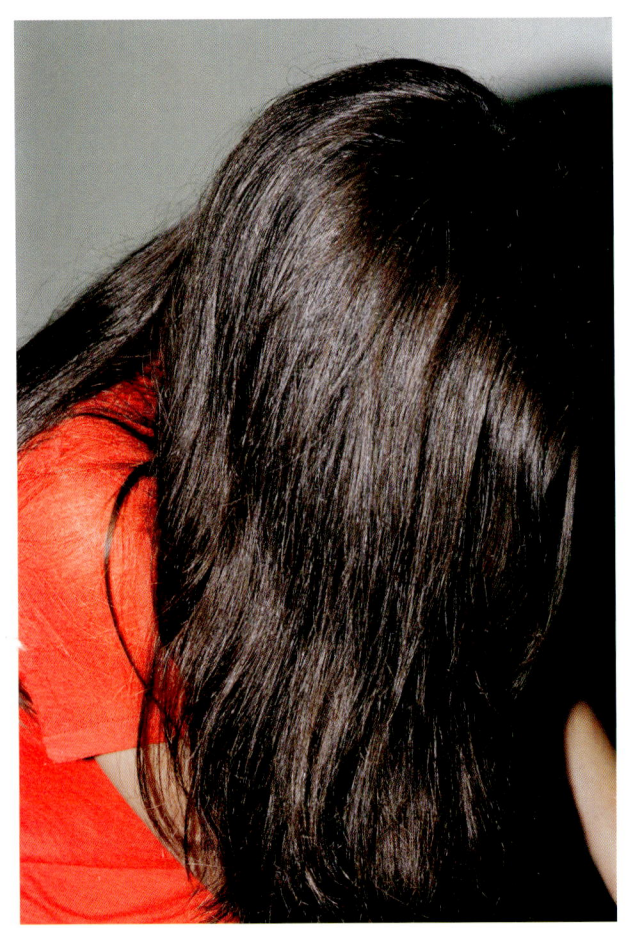
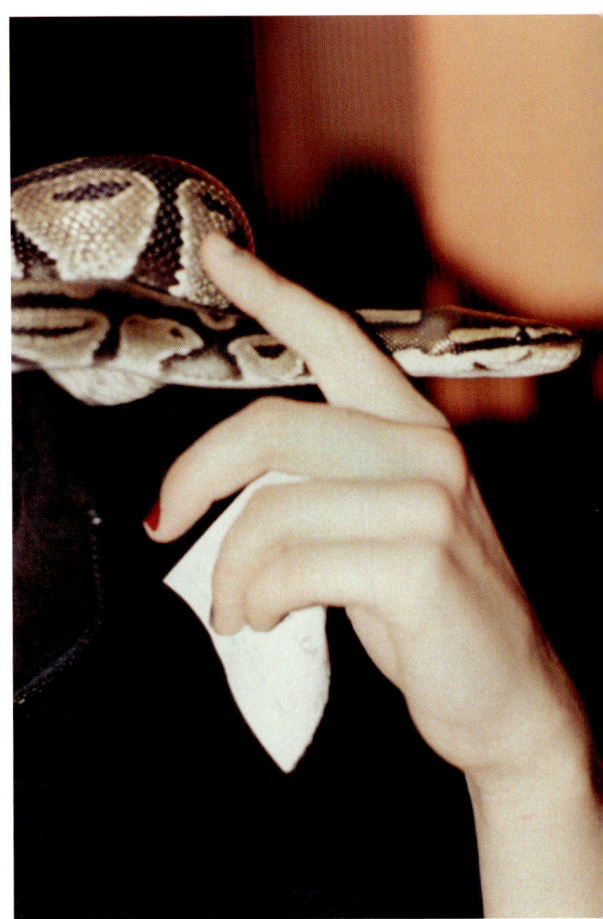

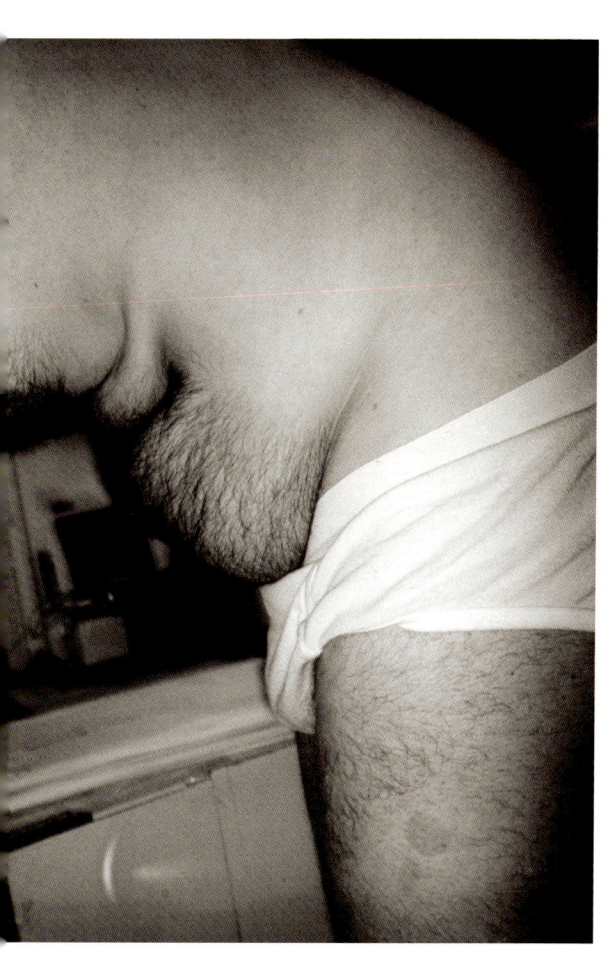
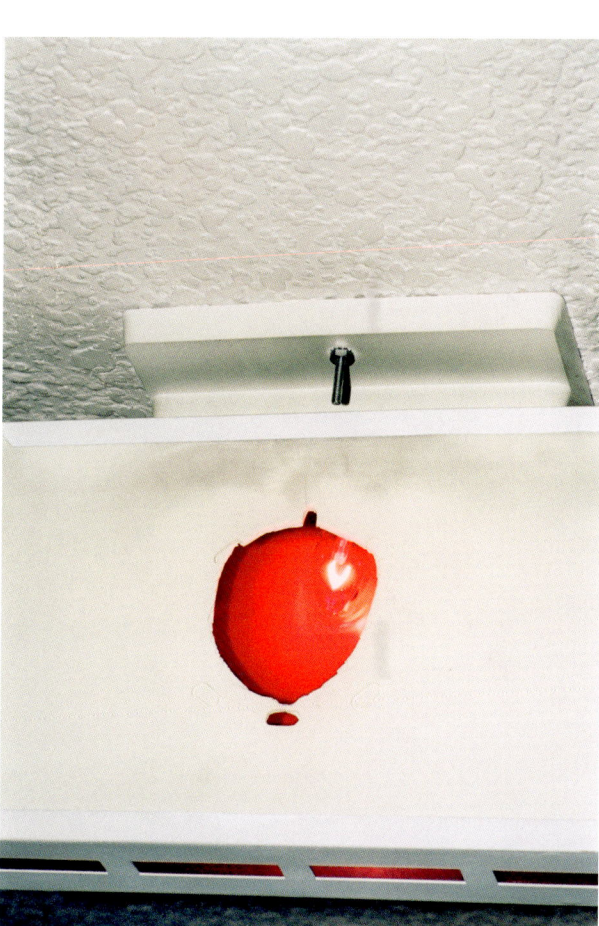

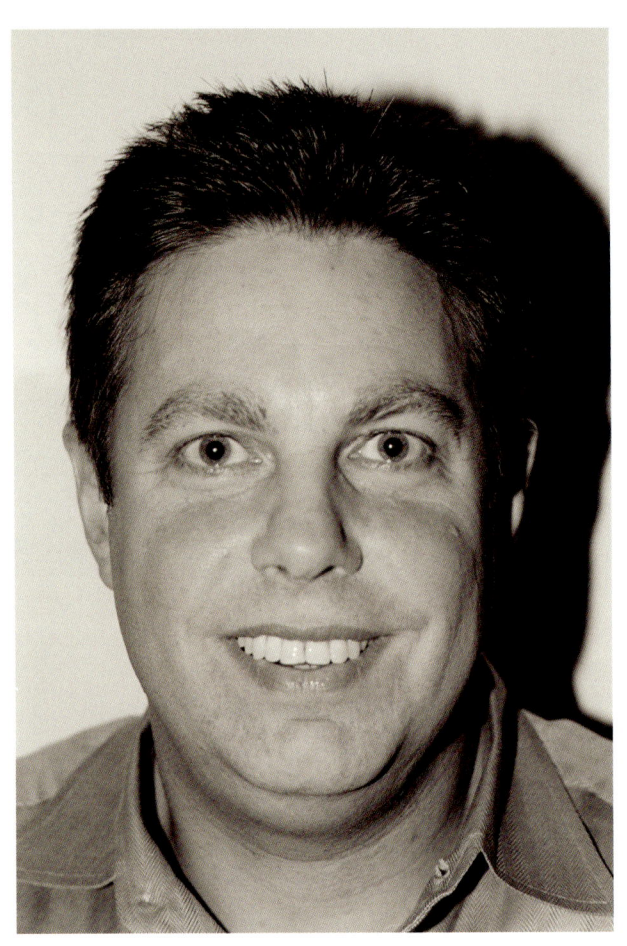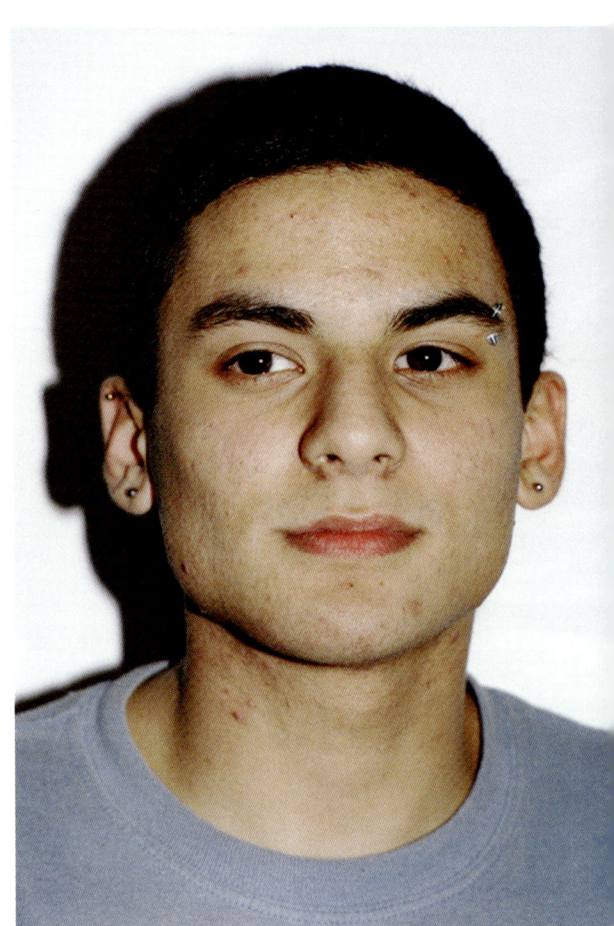

There was him,
and there was me.

There was him,
and there was me.

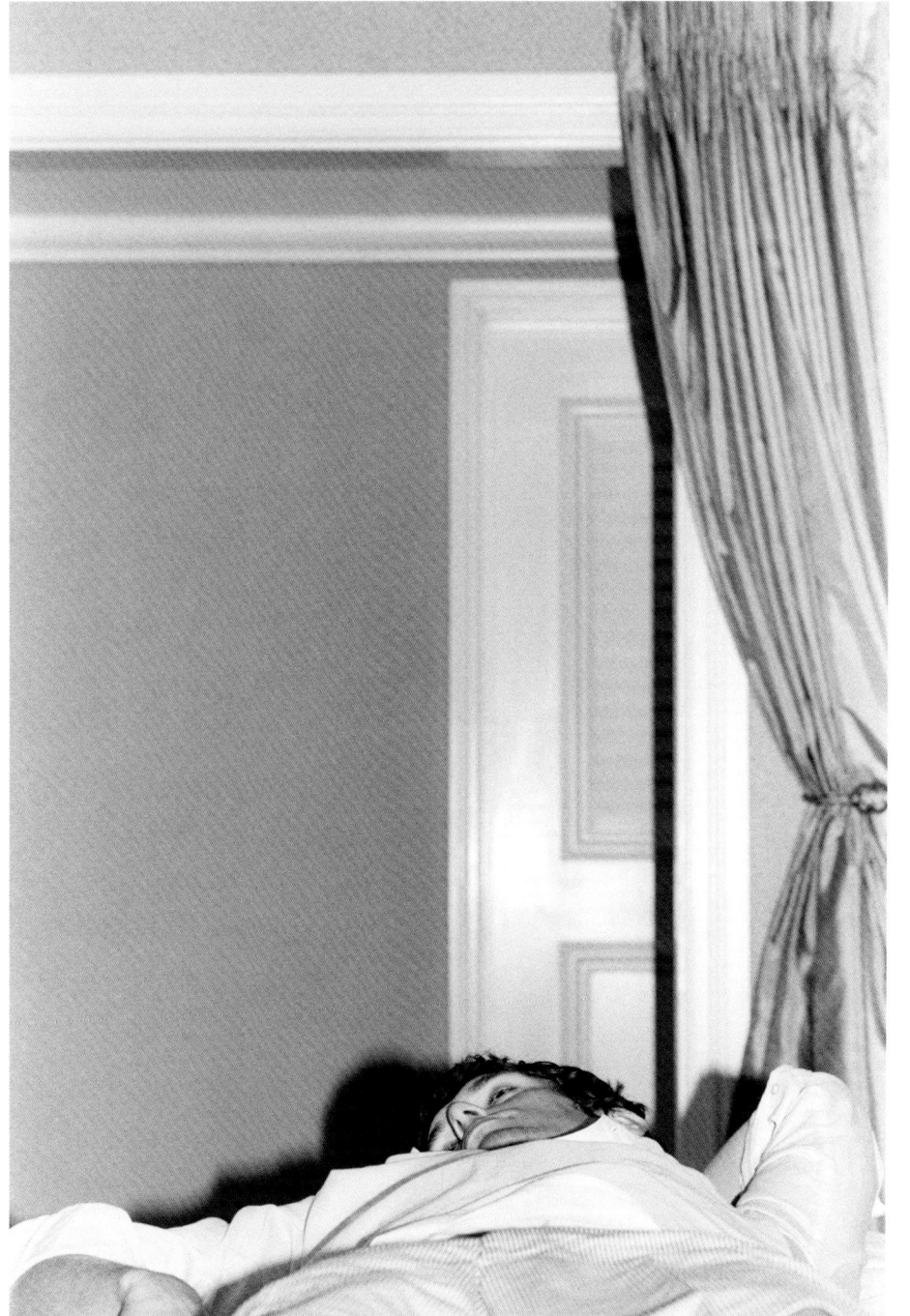

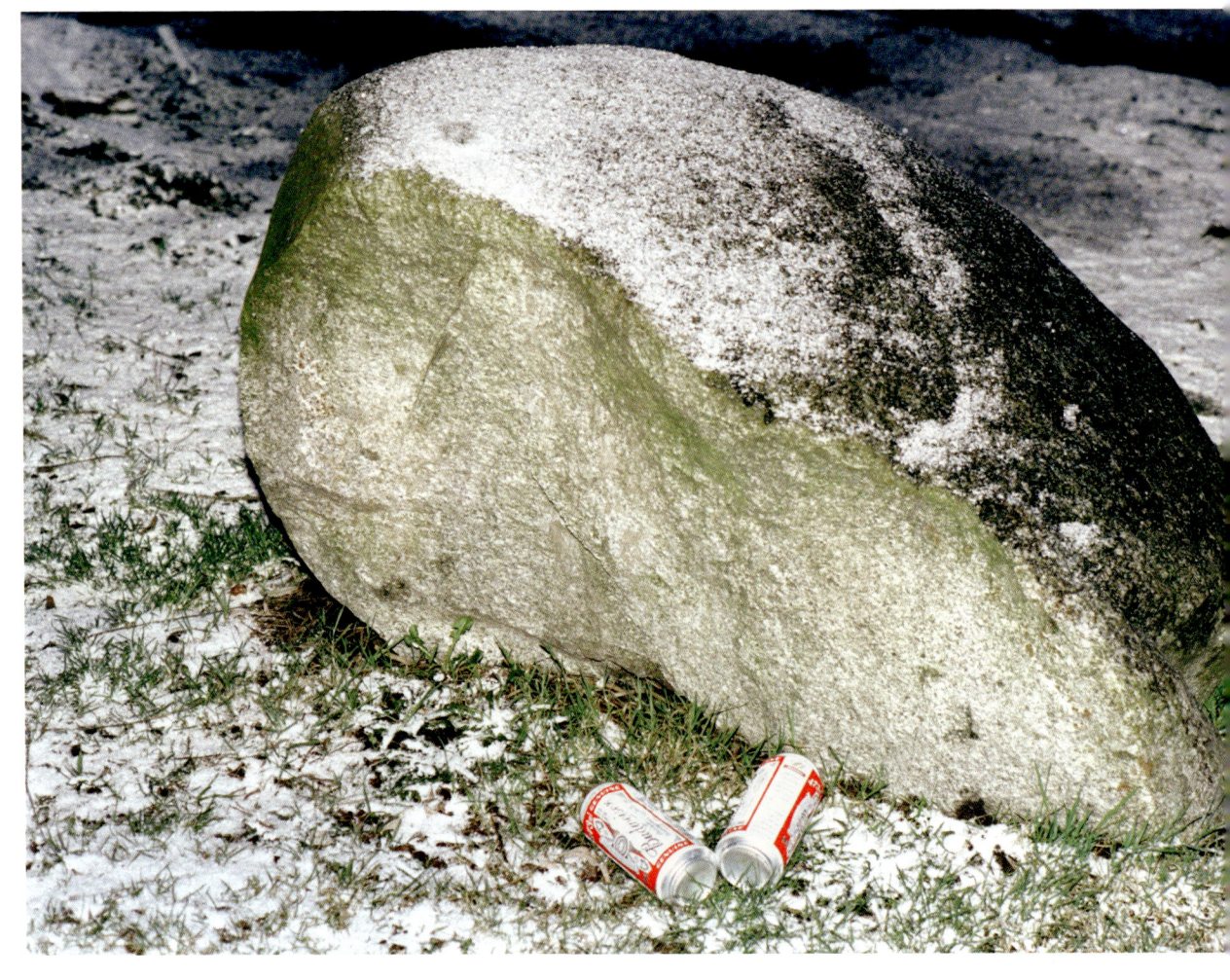

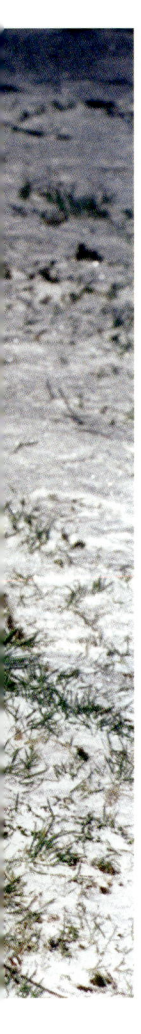

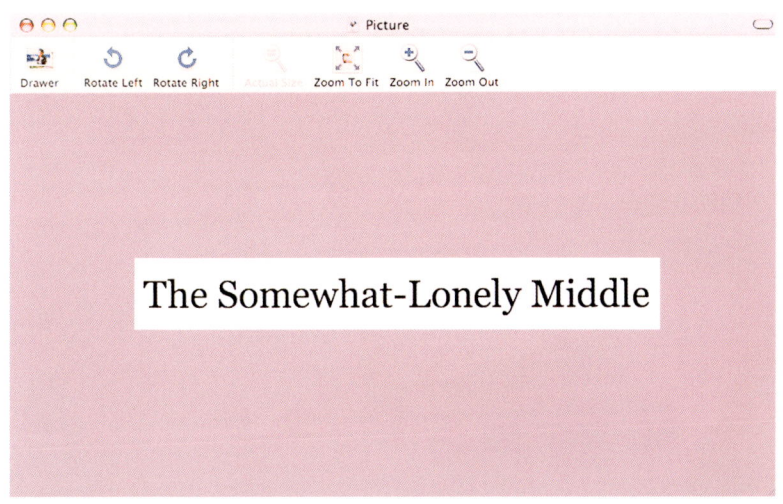

The Somewhat-Lonely Middle

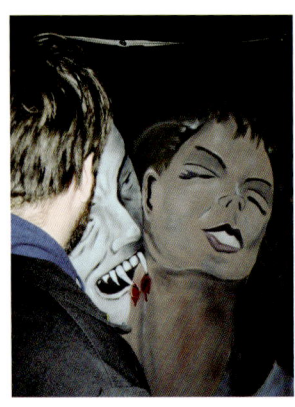
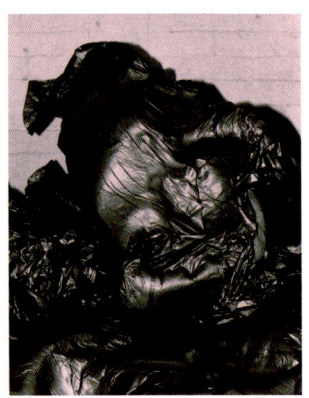
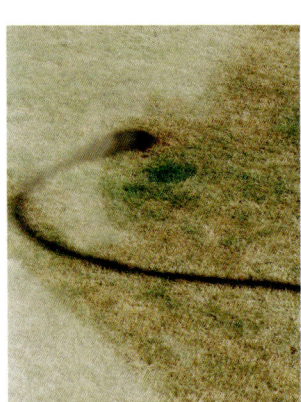
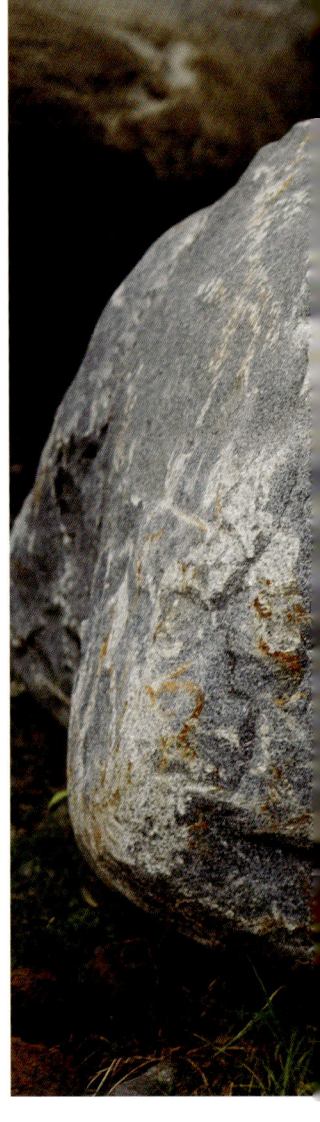
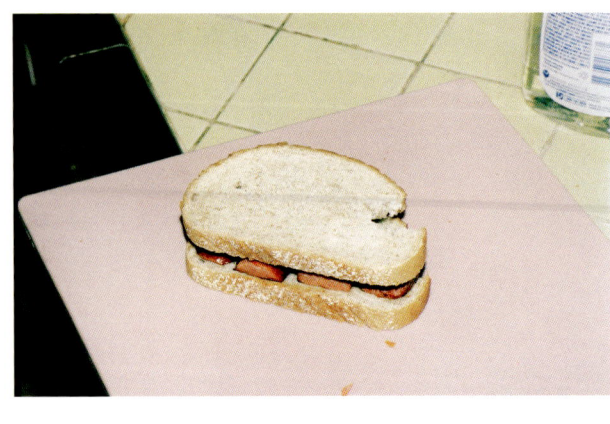

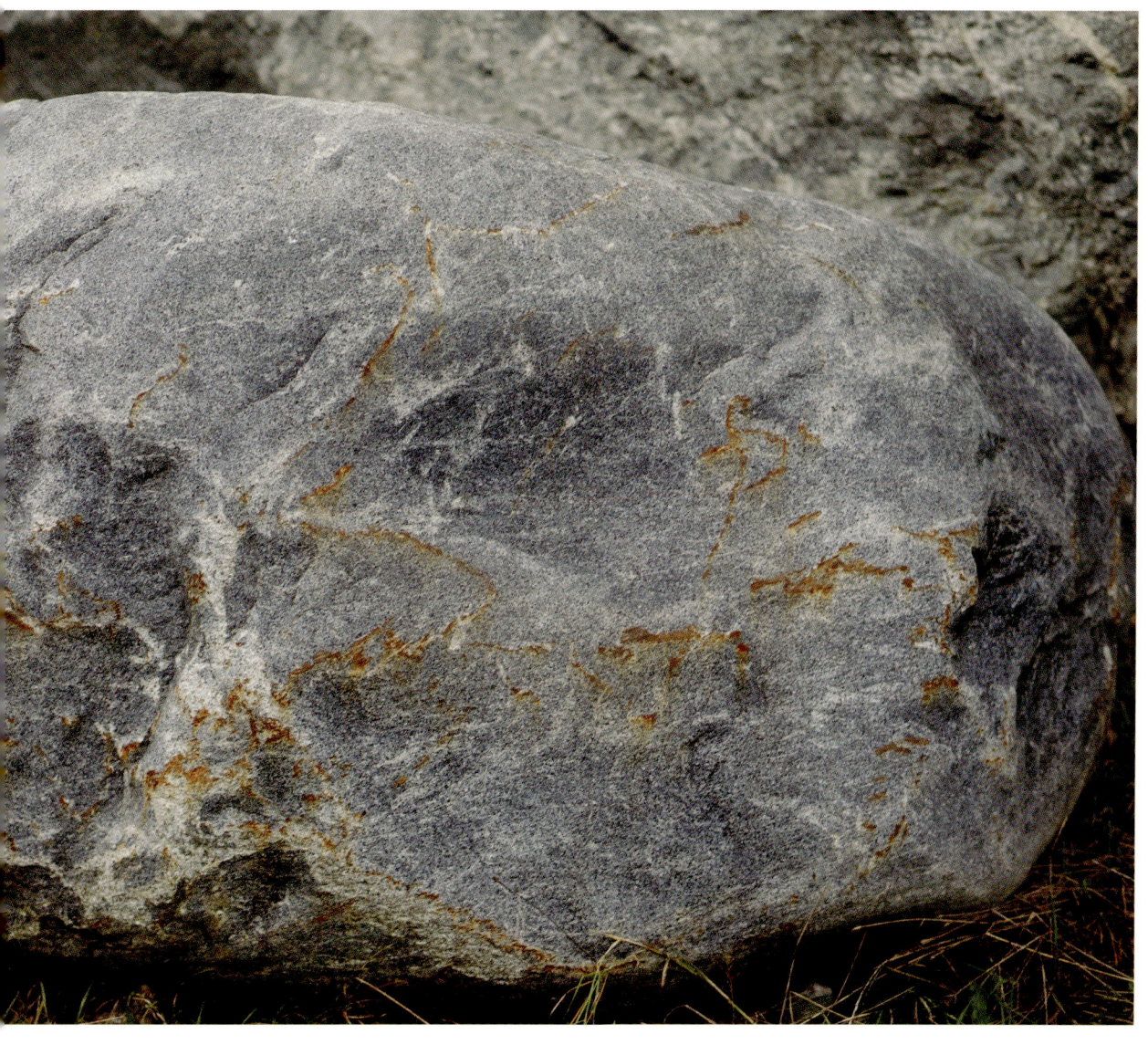

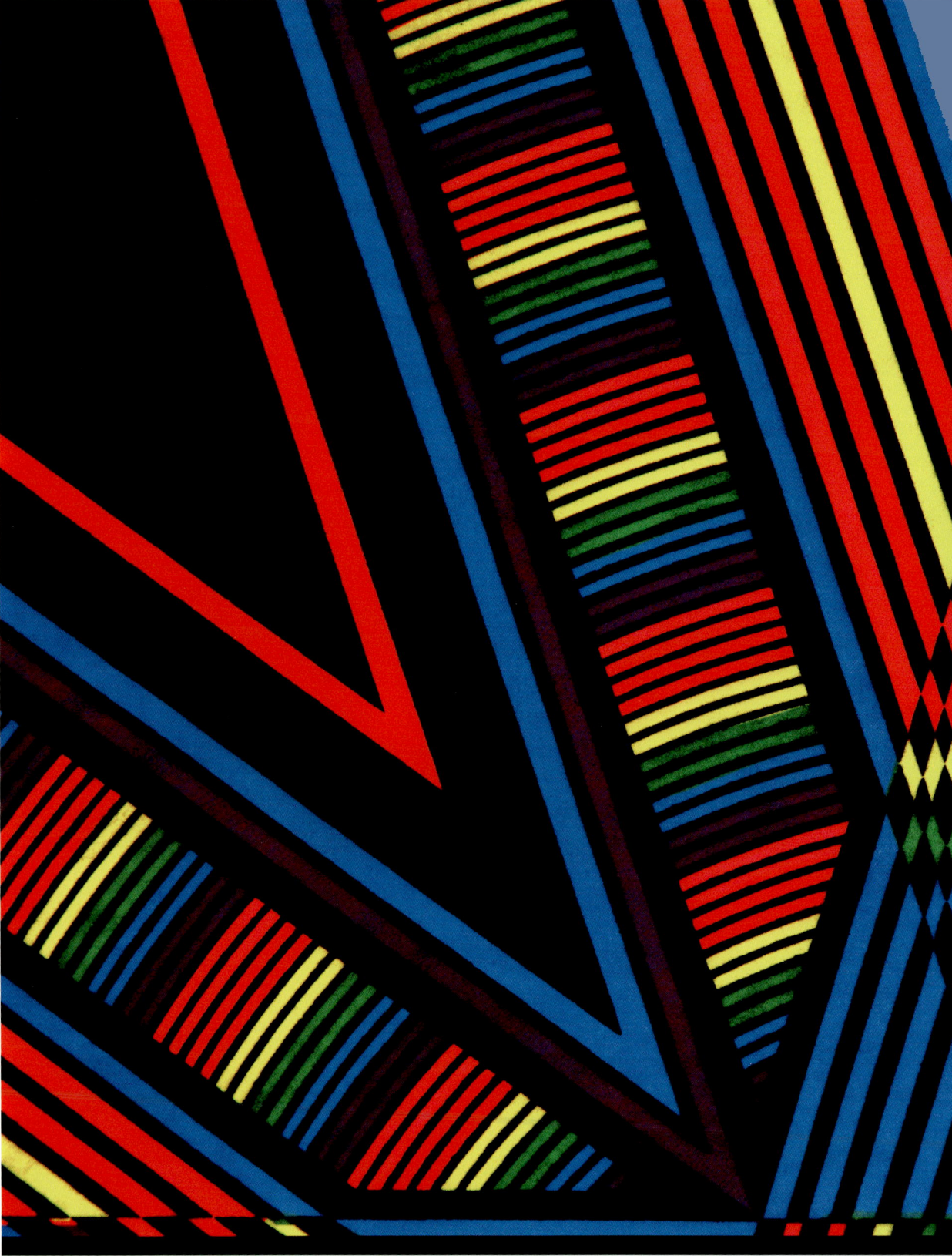

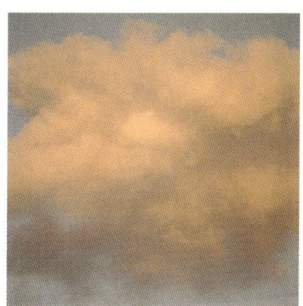

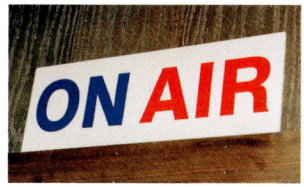

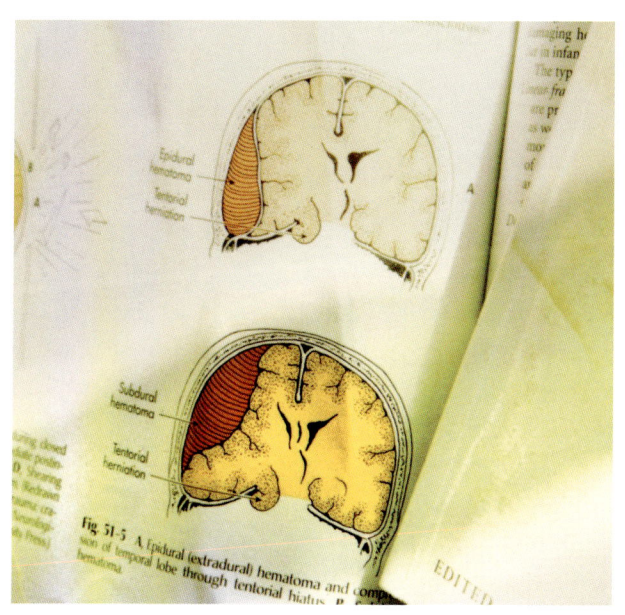

Fig 51-5 A Epidural (extradural) hematoma and comp... sion of temporal lobe through tentorial hiatus. B hematoma.

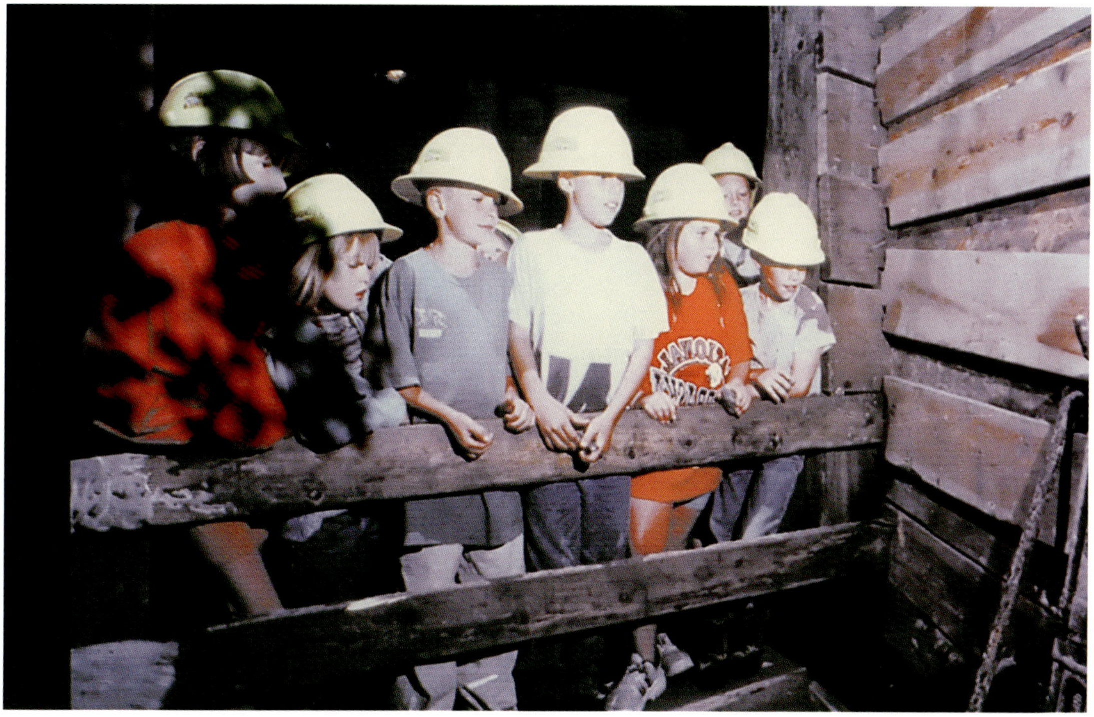

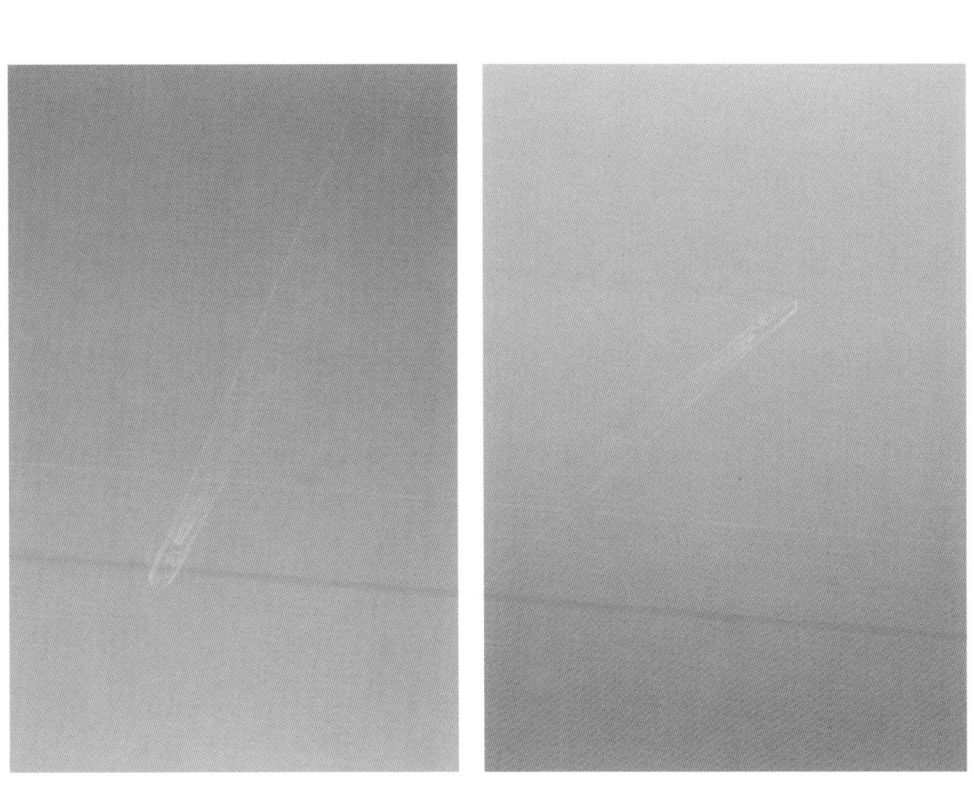

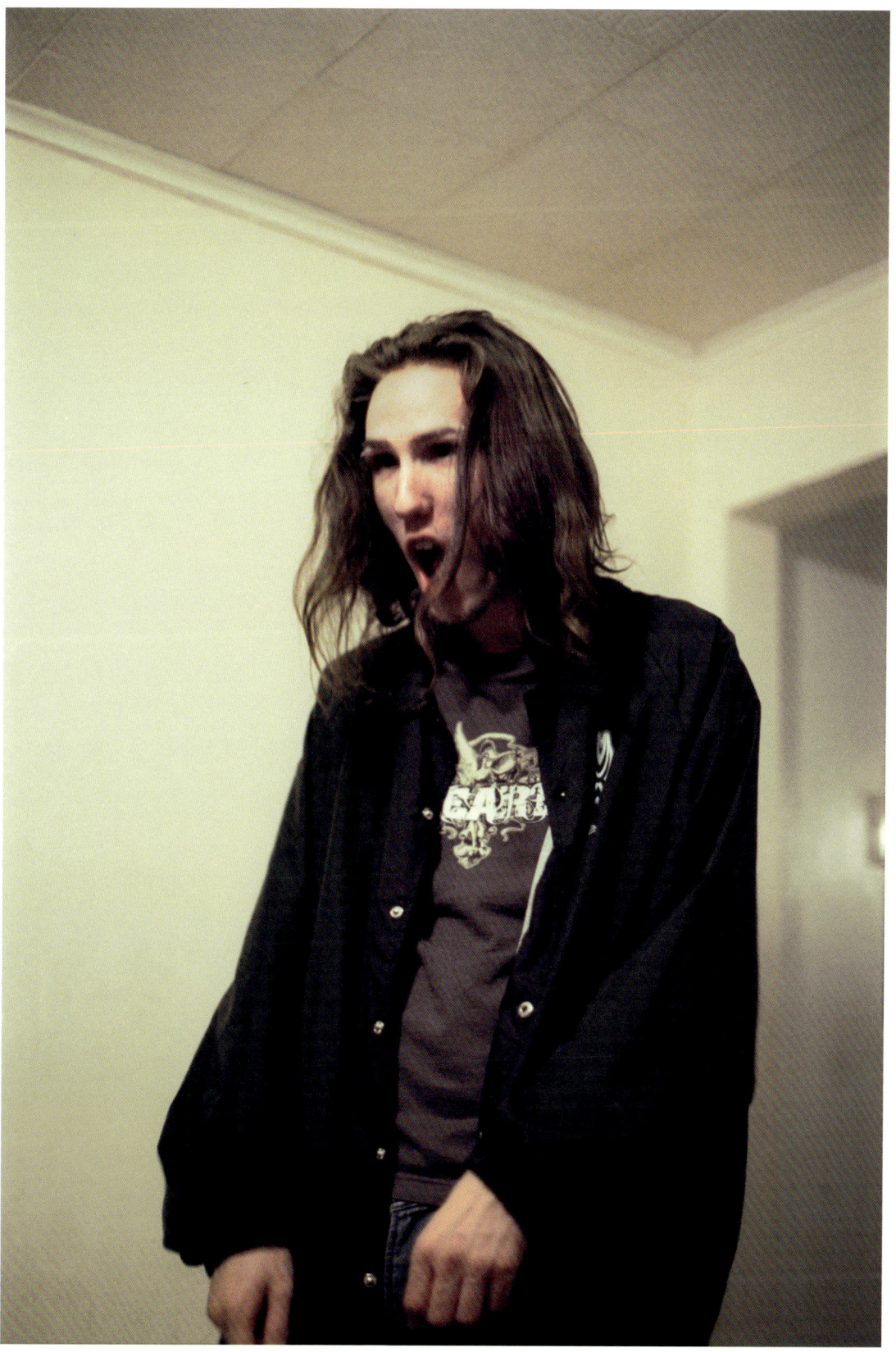

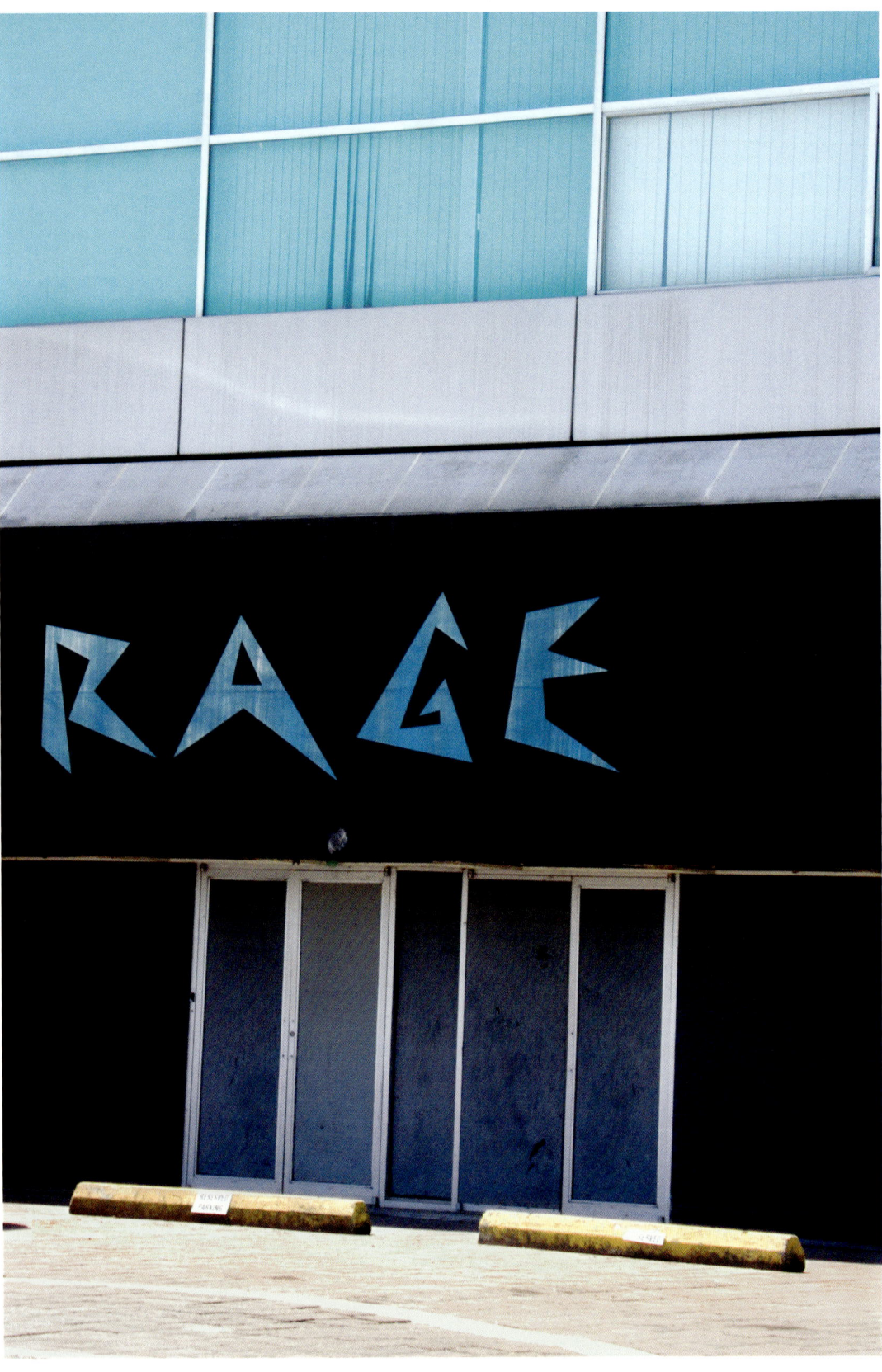

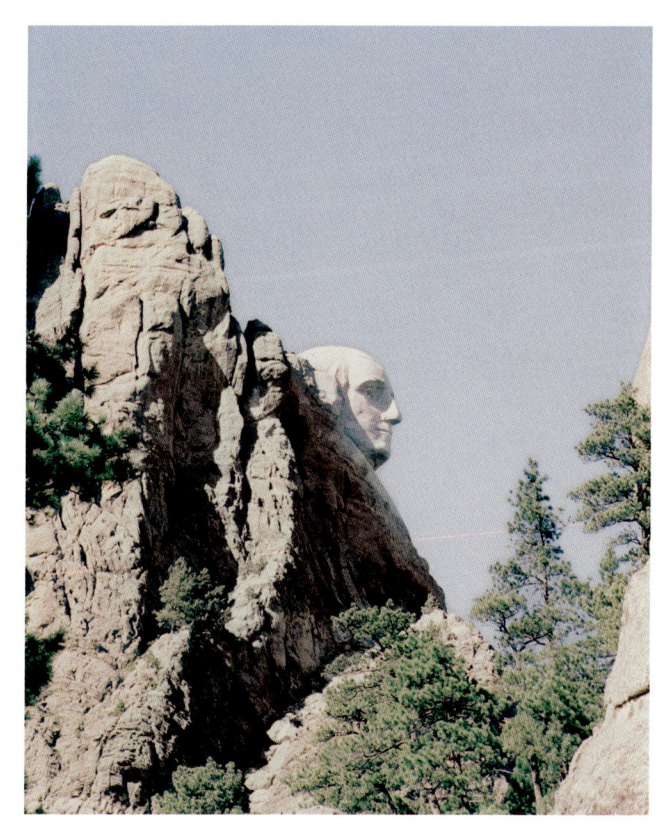

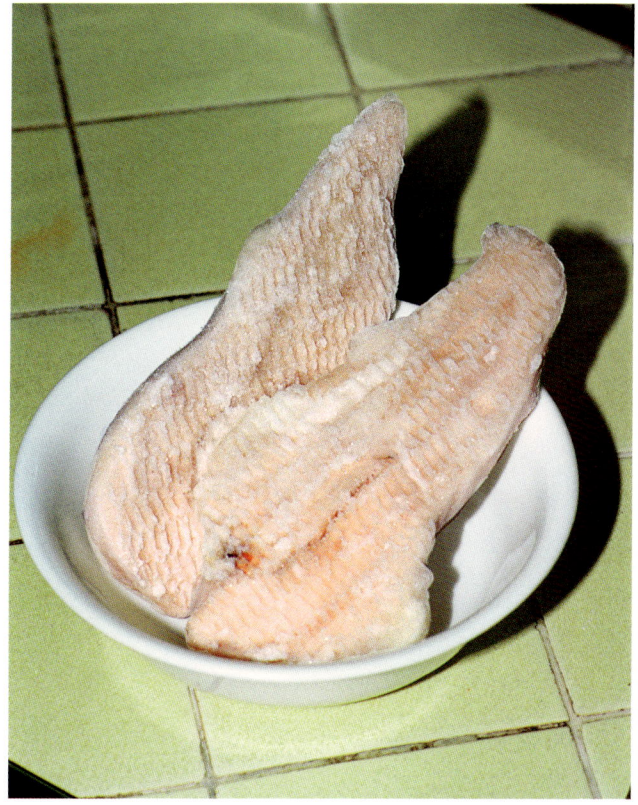

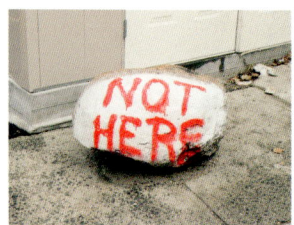

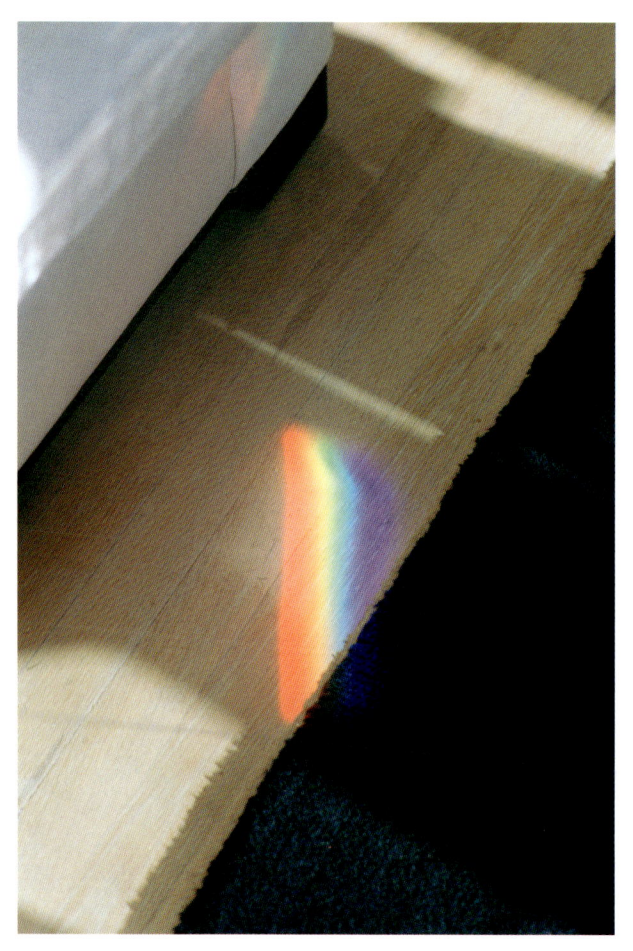

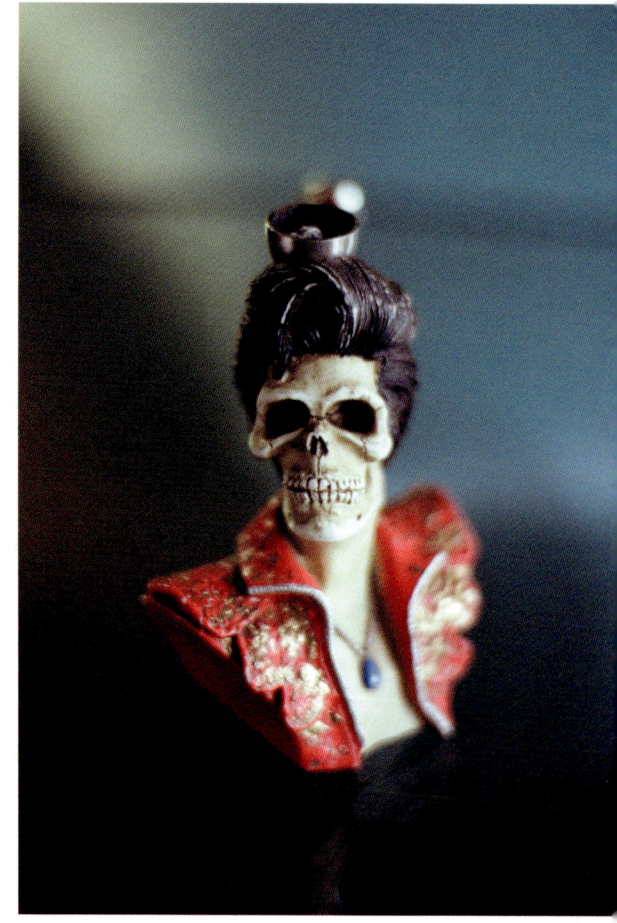

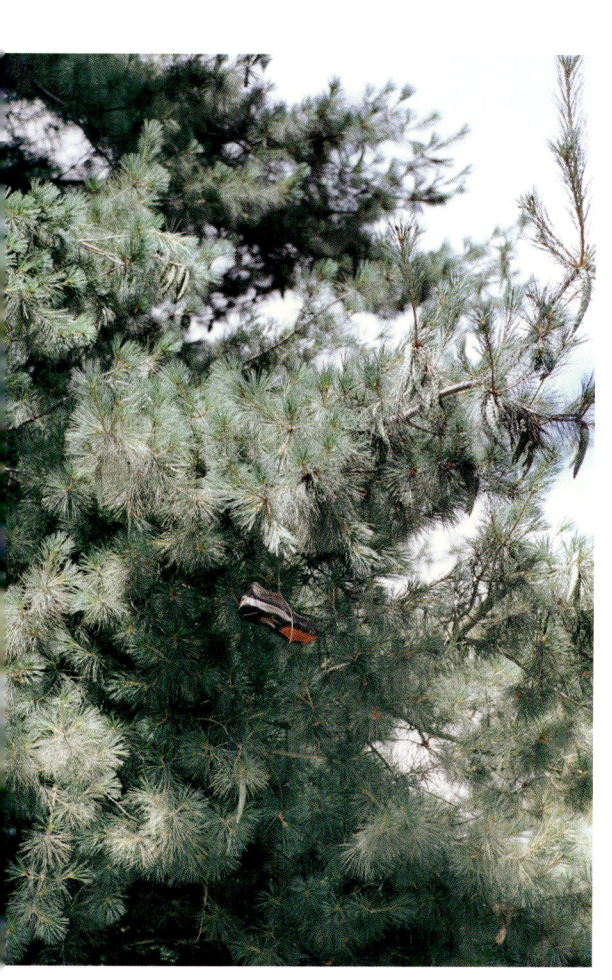
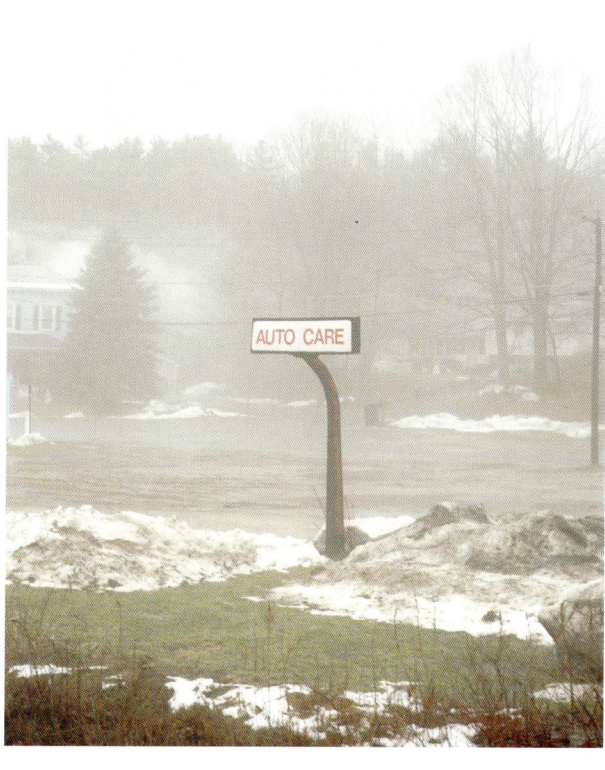

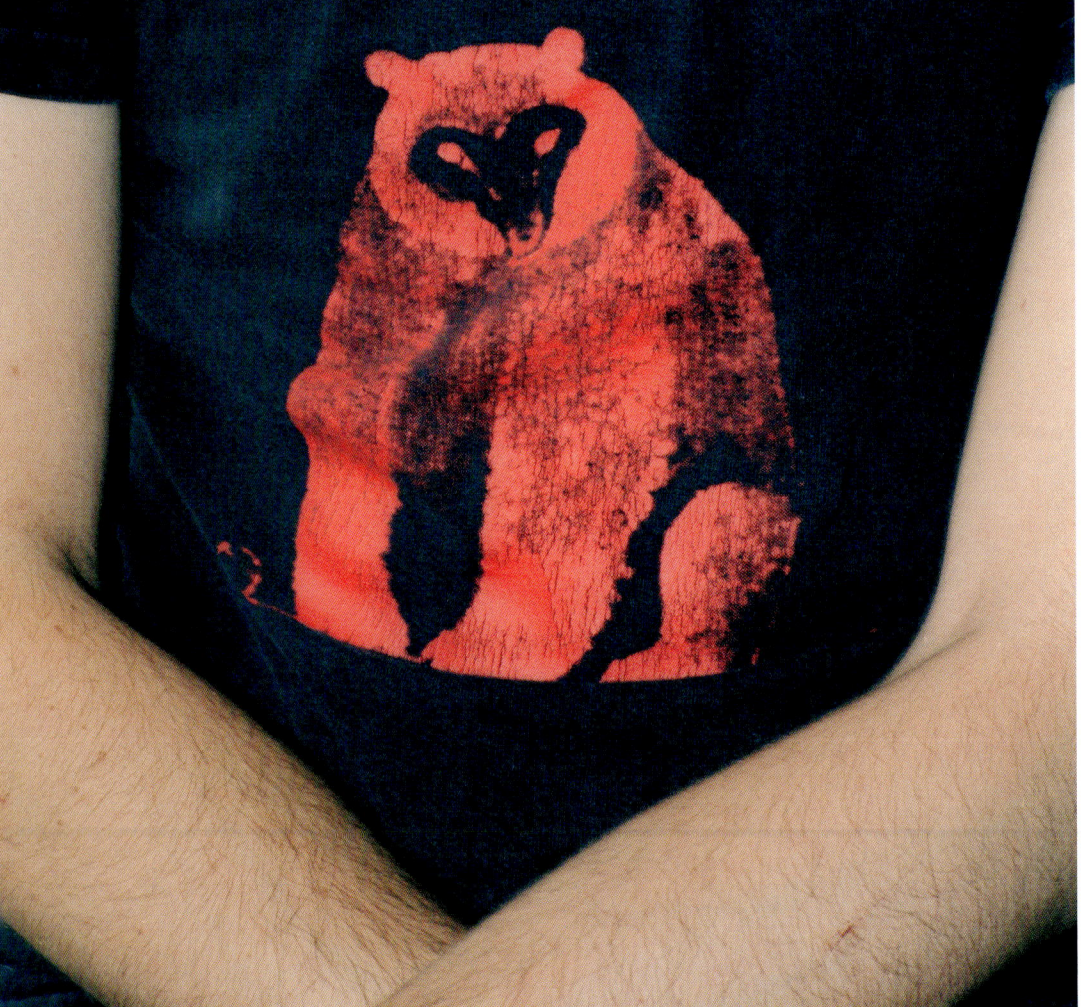

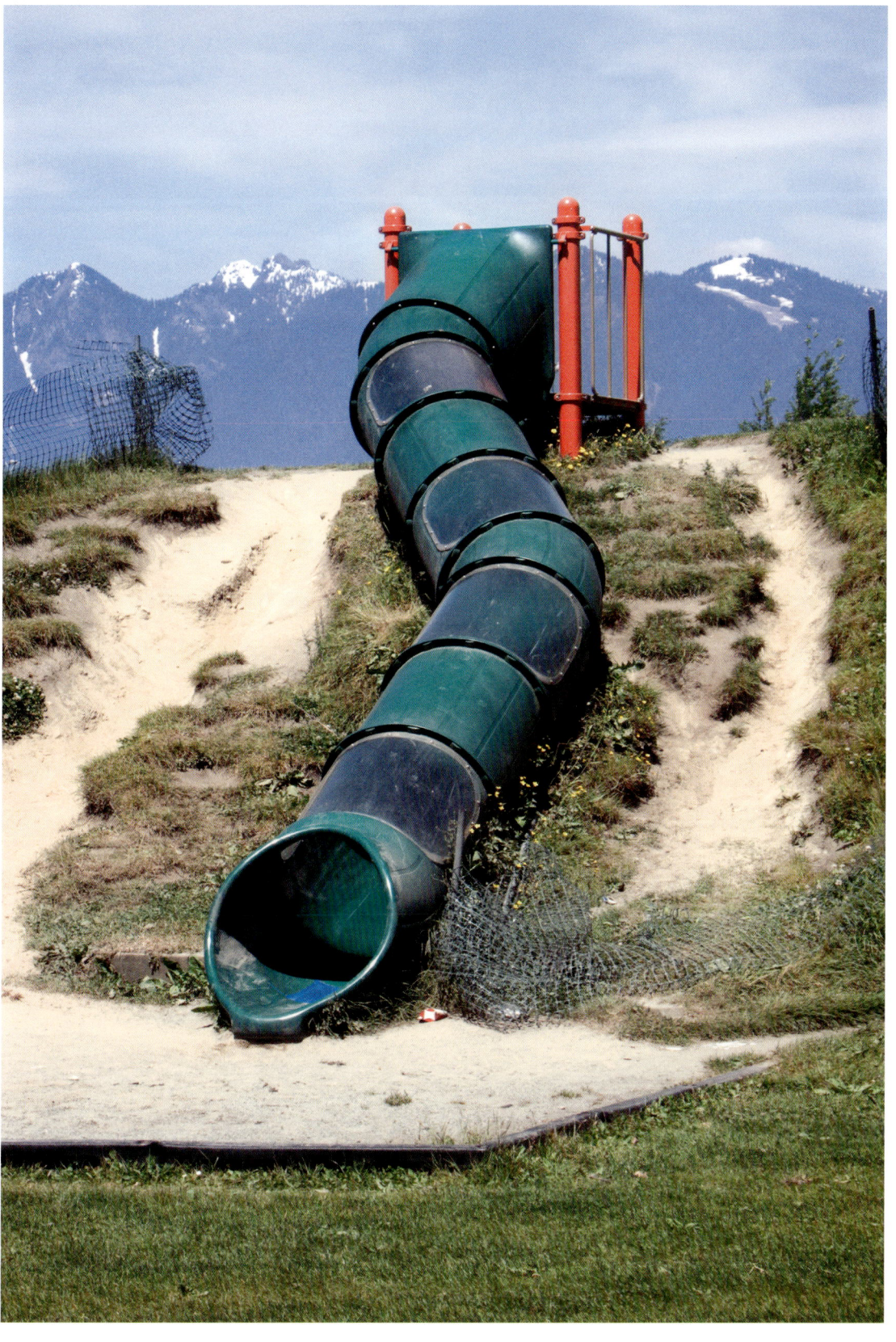

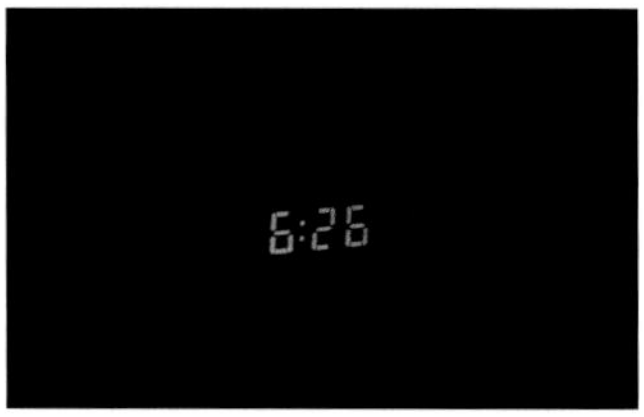
6:26

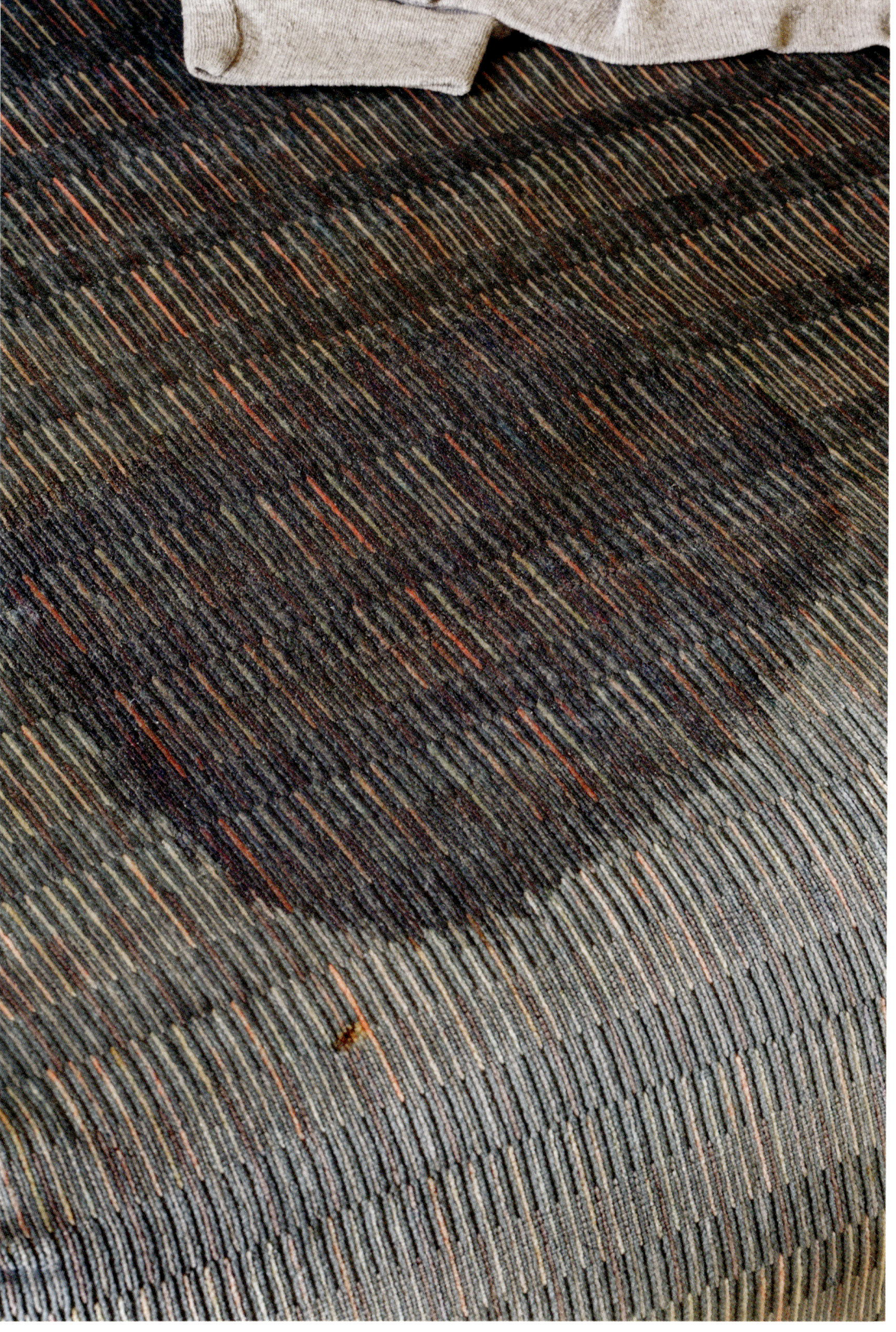

It's Over, Pt. 1
It's Over, Pt. 2
It's Love
Is It Over
I Know It's Over
Admit It's Over
Again It's Over
It's over Again
It's Over There
Get over It
War Is Over
It's Not over Yet
Before It's Over
It's Over Skinny!
Don't Say It's Over
Now That It's Over

It's Over Man
It's Over, Pt. 3
It's over, Sid
Don't Dream It's Over
Think It Over
And When It's Over
It's over Love
After It's Over
Baby It's Over
Dove (It's Over)
Girl It's Over
Glad Its Over
It's Over & Done
It's Over, Baby
It's over, Johnny

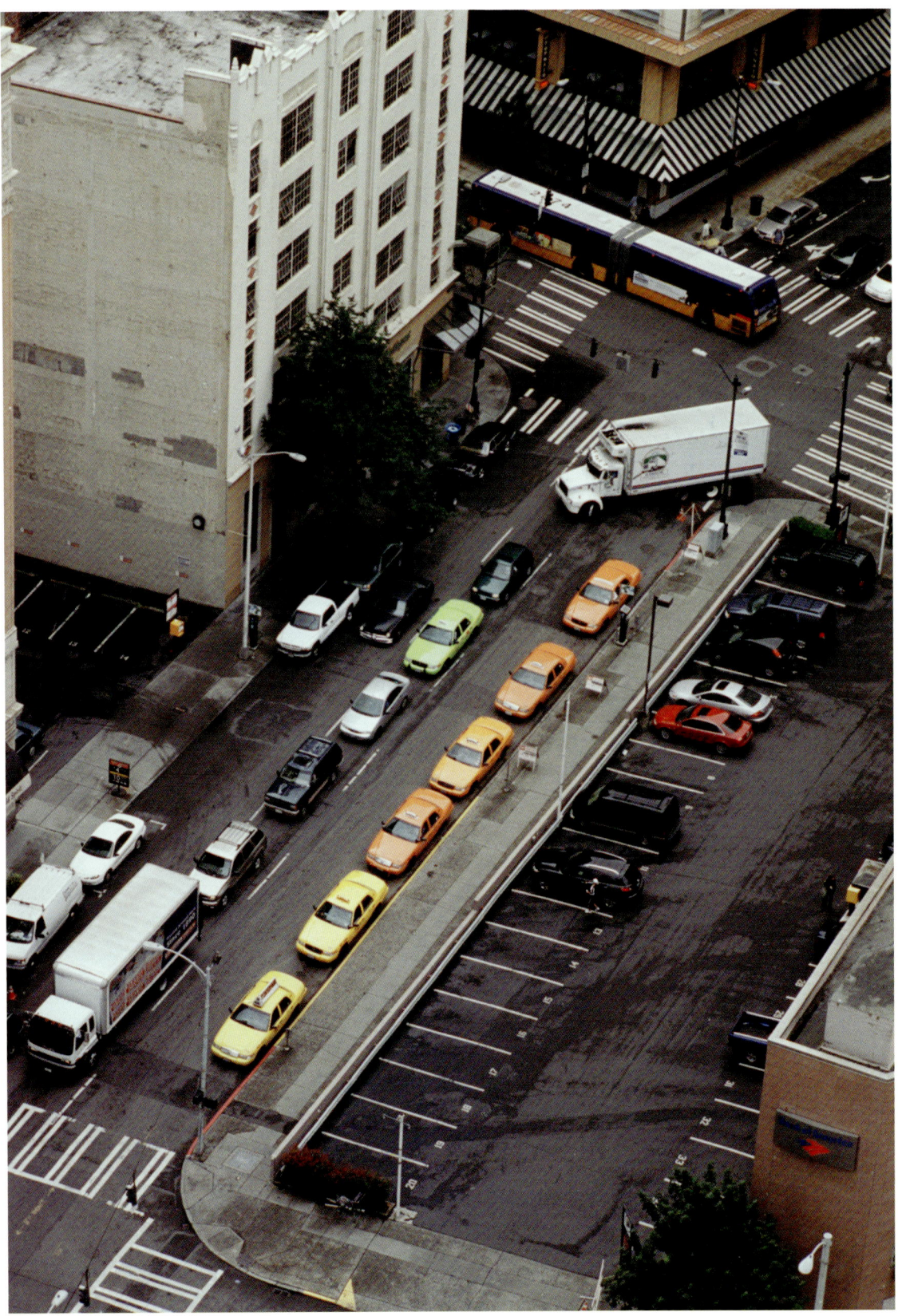

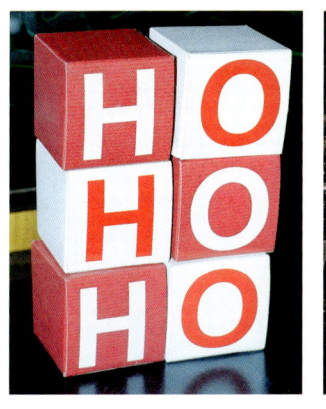
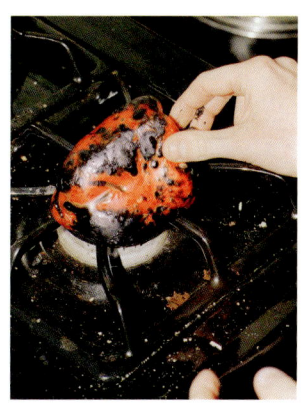
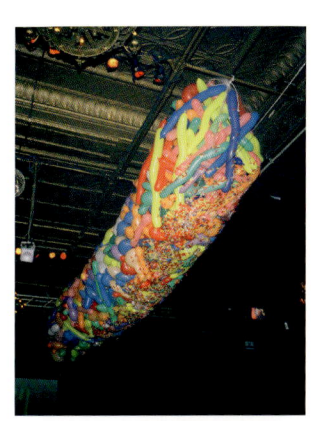
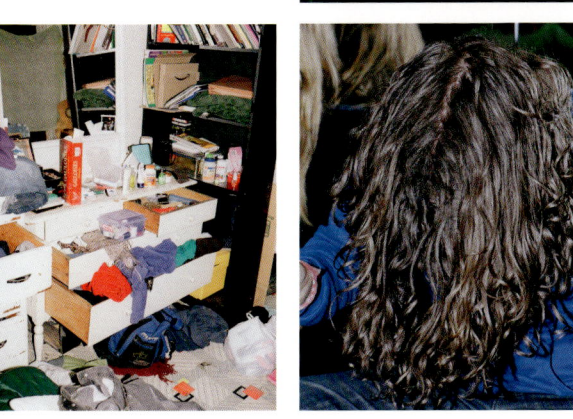
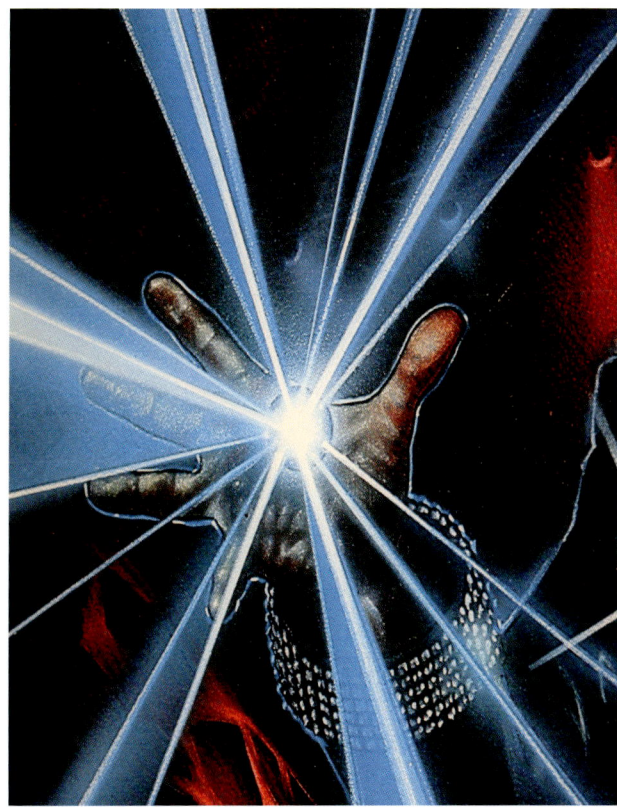

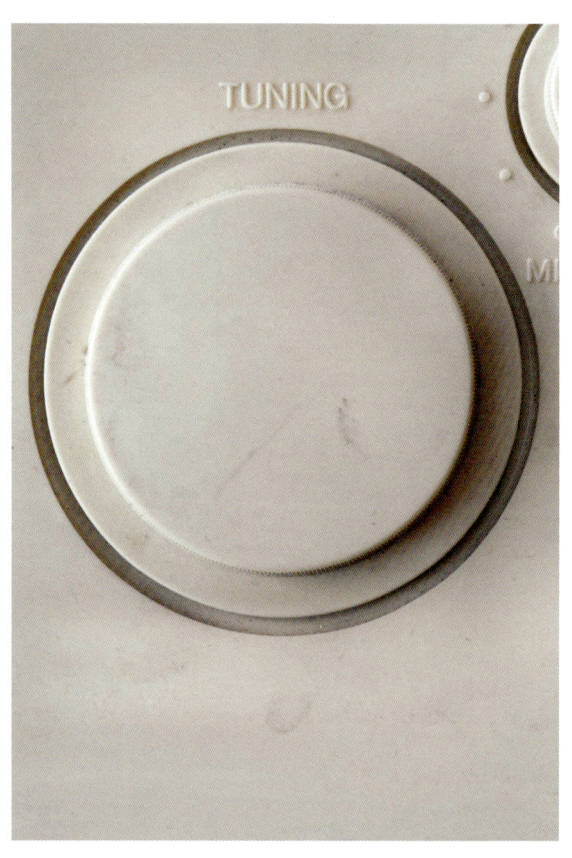

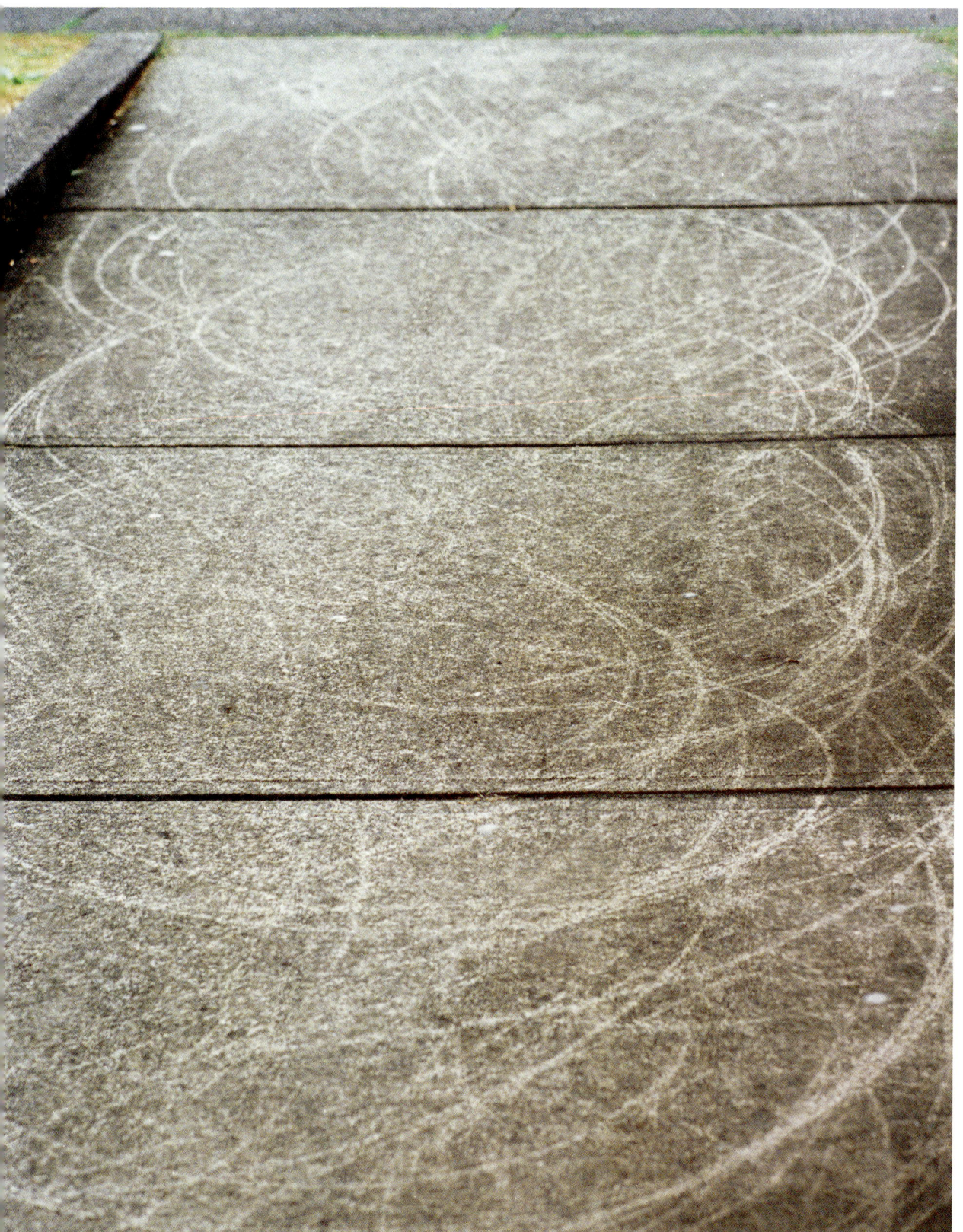

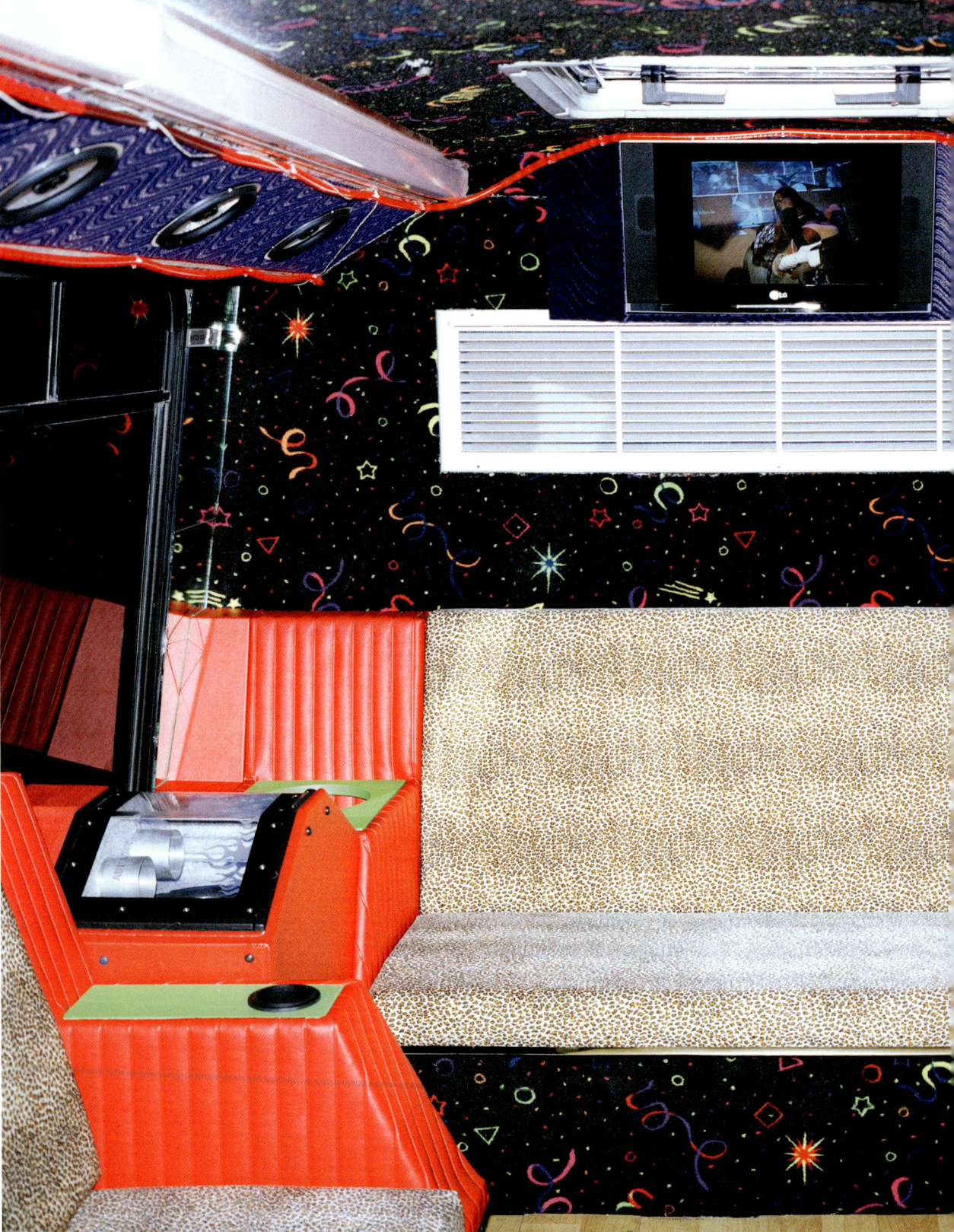

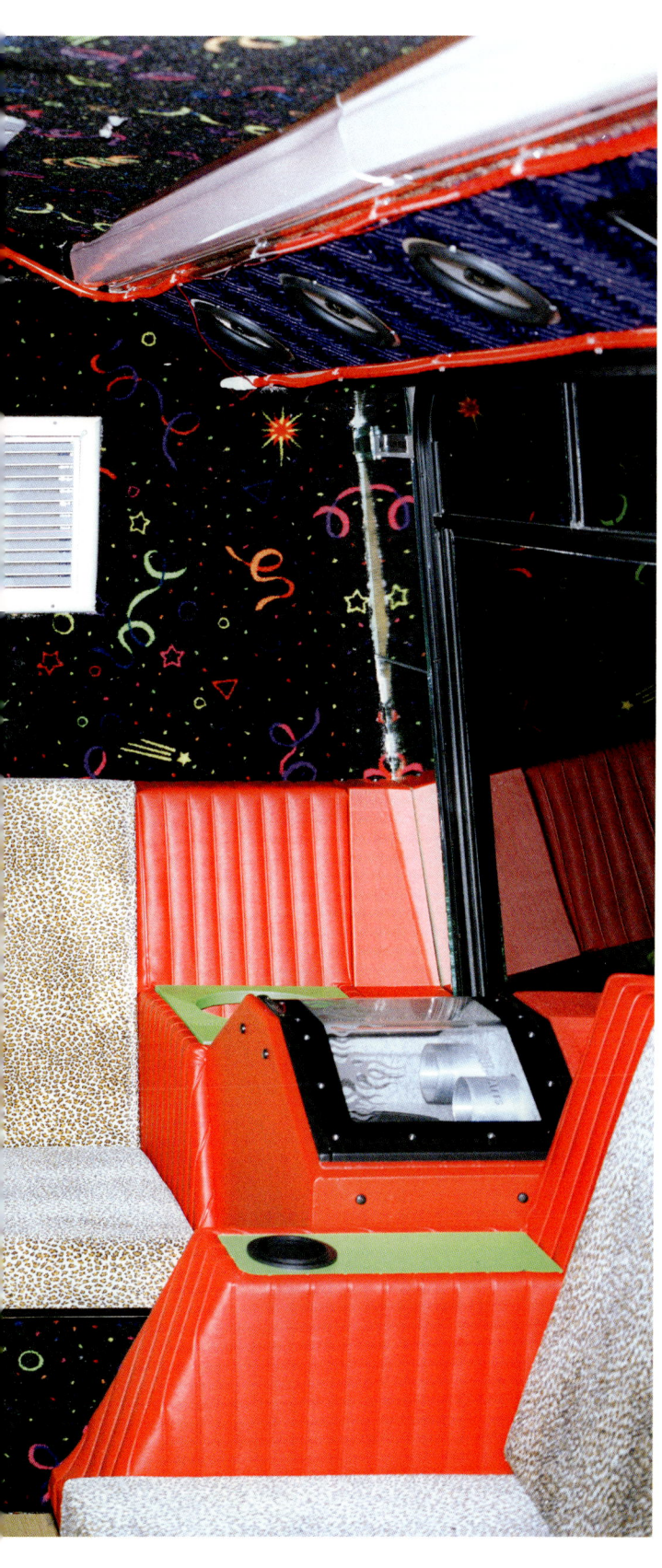

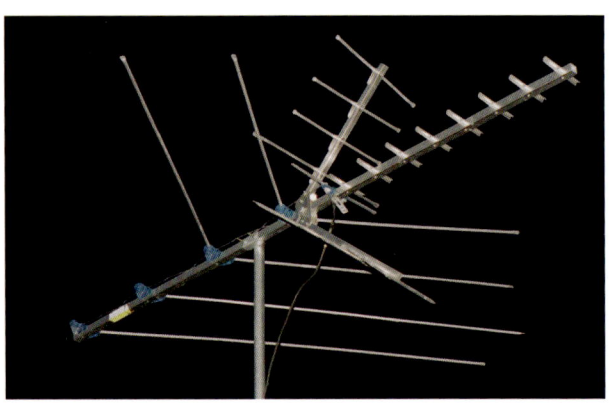

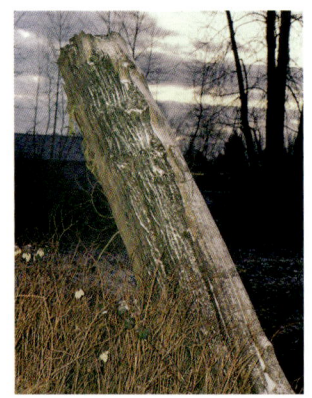

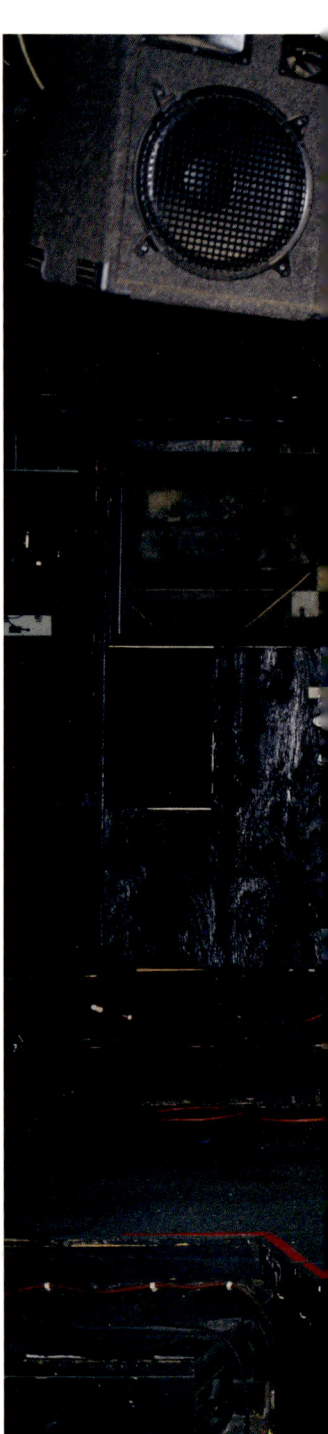

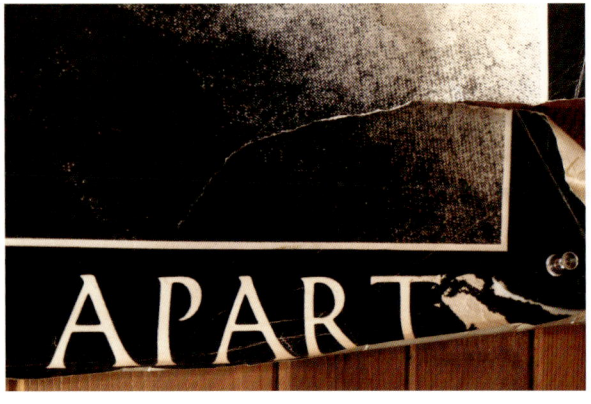

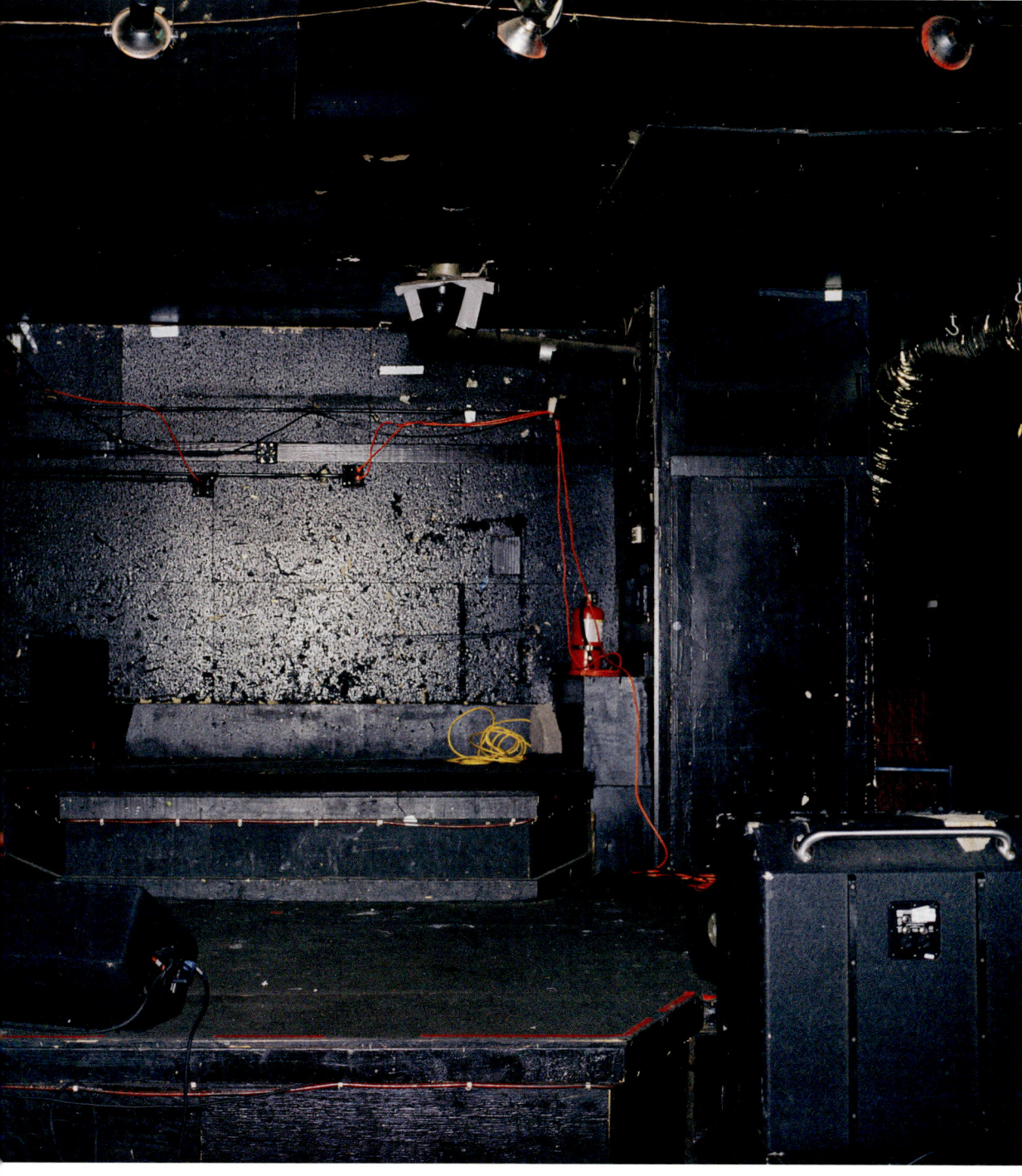

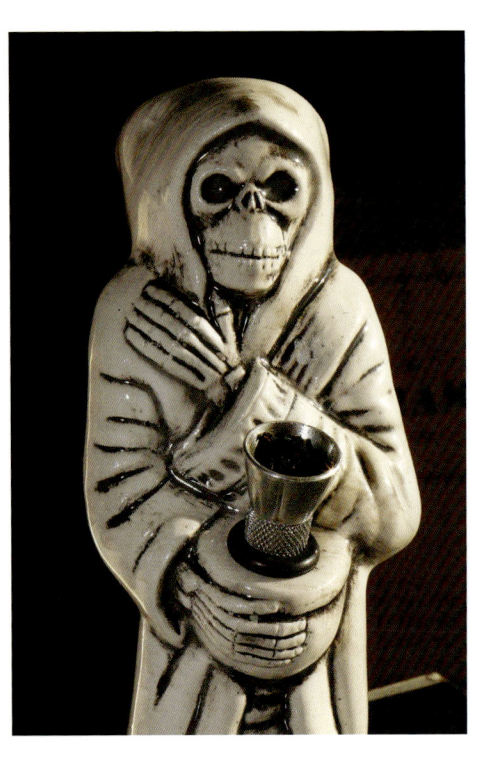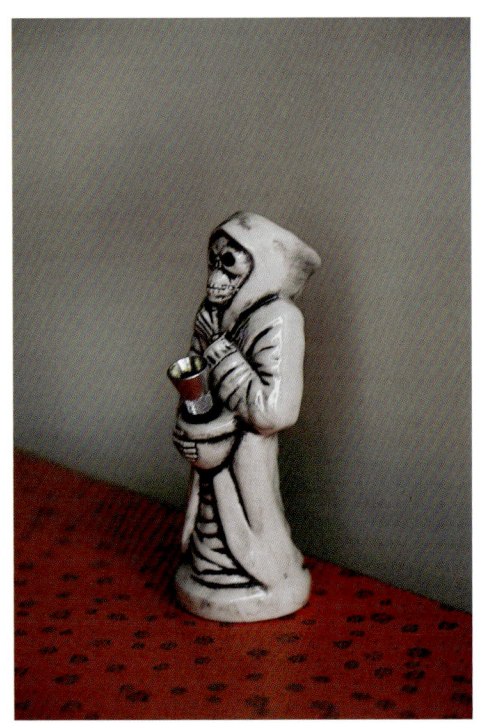

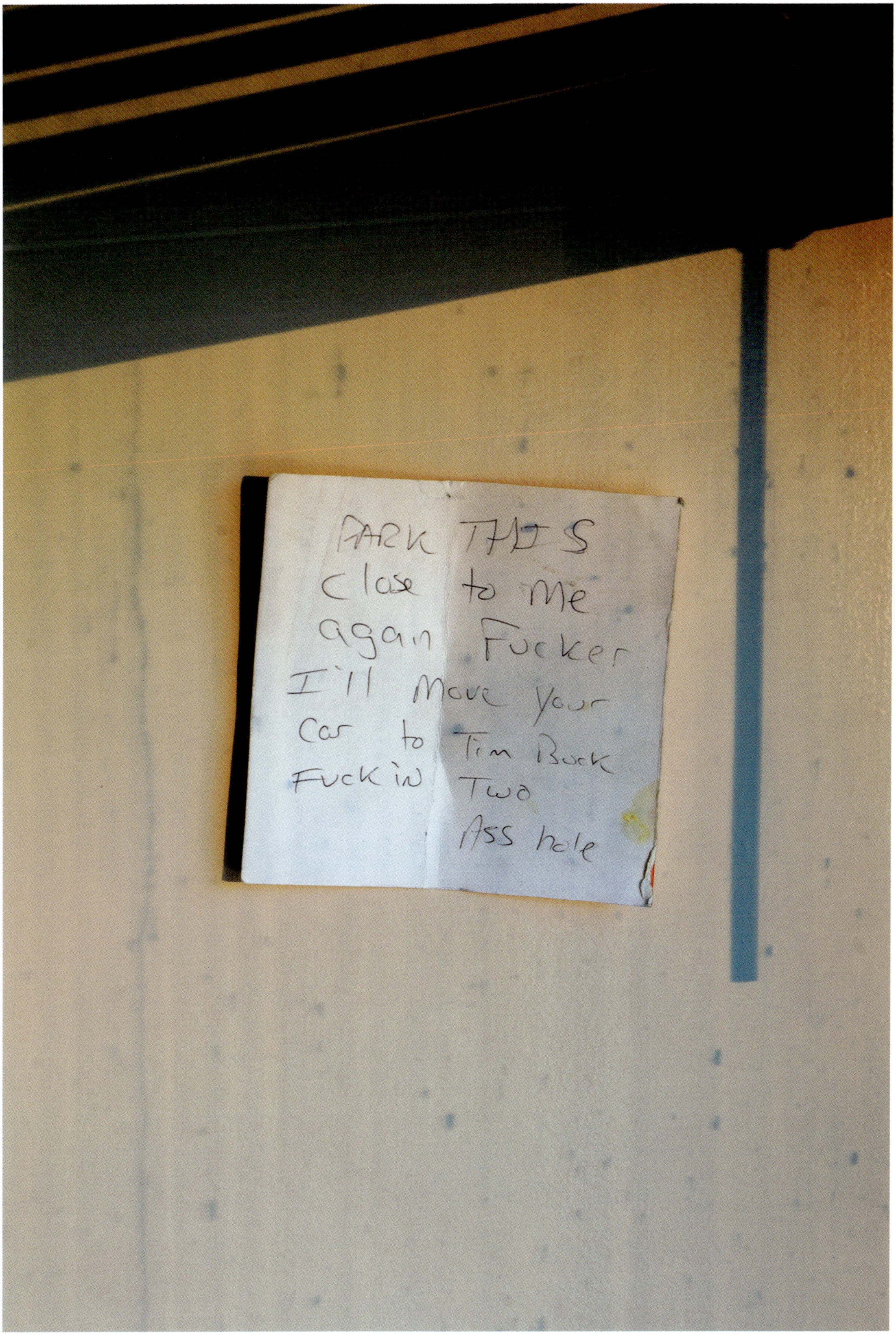
PARK THIS
close to me
again Fucker
I'll move your
car to Tim Buck
Fuckin Two
Ass hole

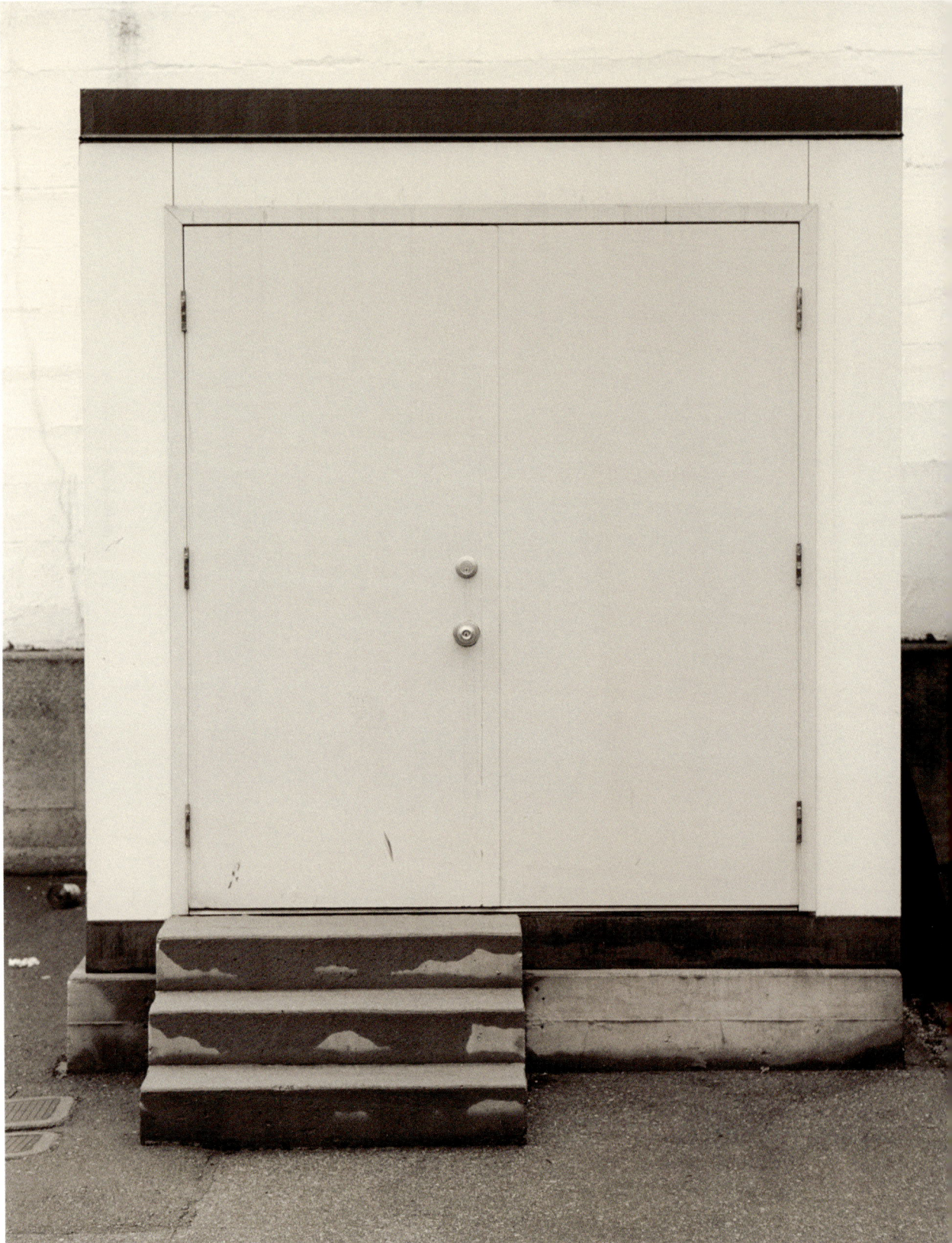

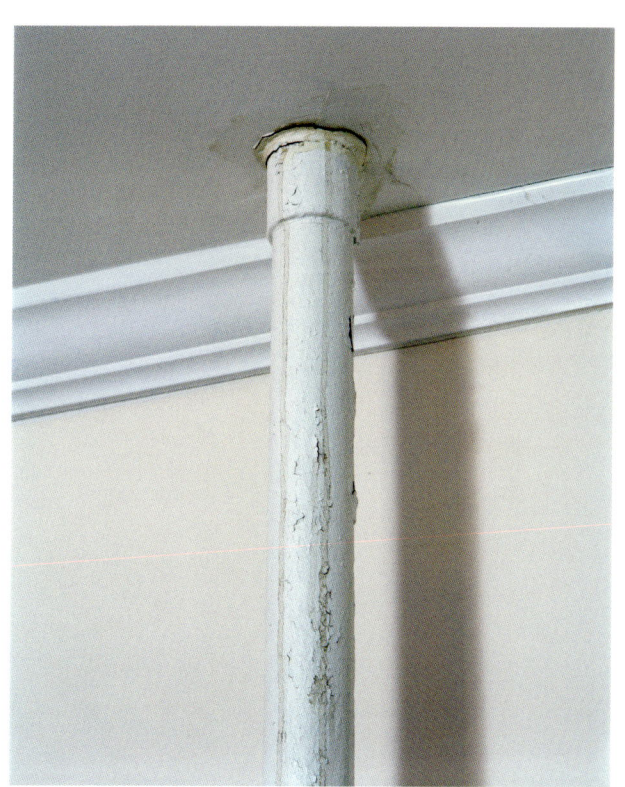

"a shot in the arm,"

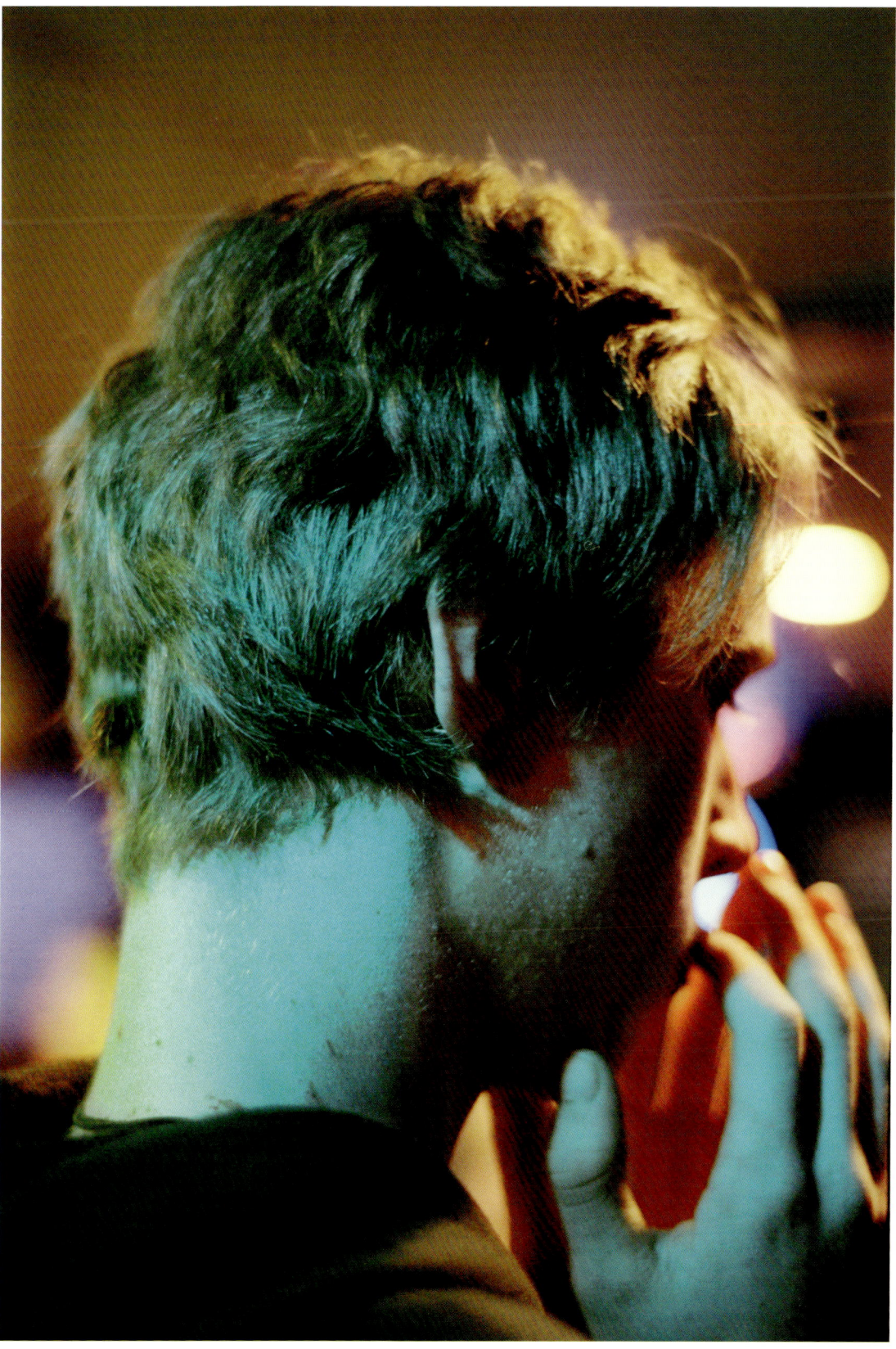

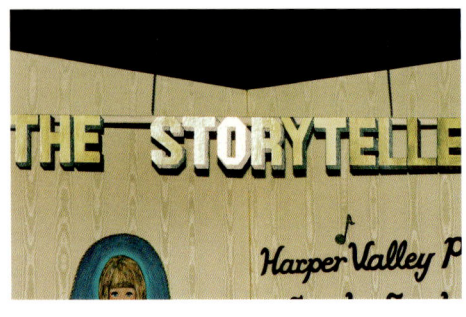

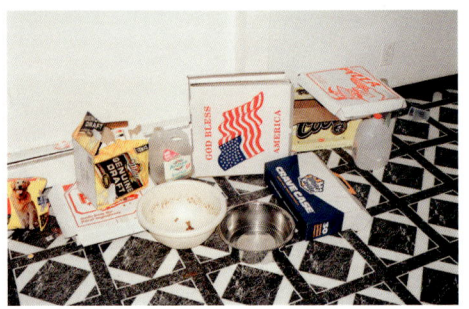

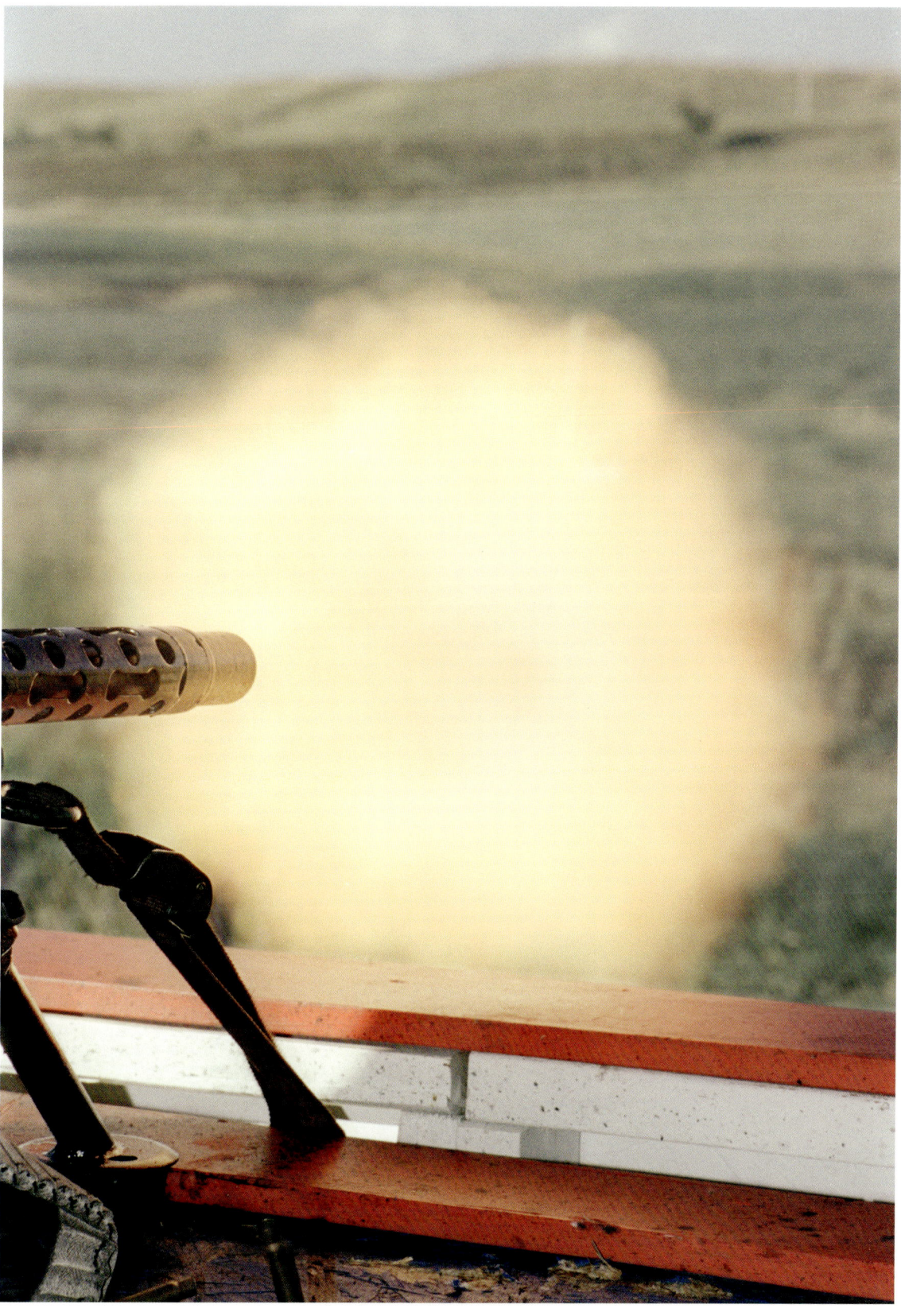

Good googly moogly, that thang is juicy
Good googly moogly, that thang is juicy
Good googly moogly, that thang is juicy
Good googly moogly, that thang is juicy
Good googly moogly, that thang is juicy
Good googly moogly, that thang is juicy
Good googly moogly, that thang is juicy
Good googly moogly, that thang is juicy

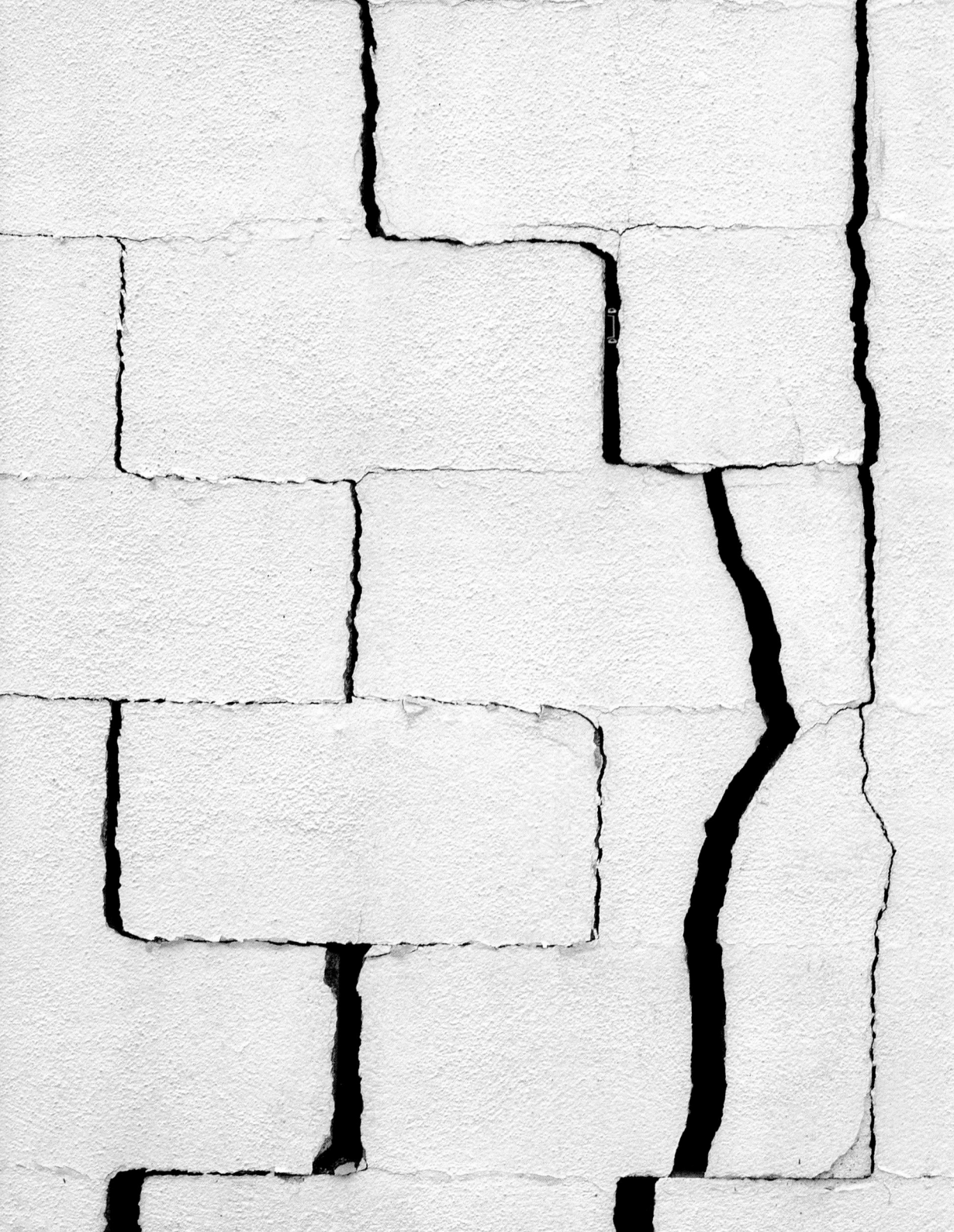

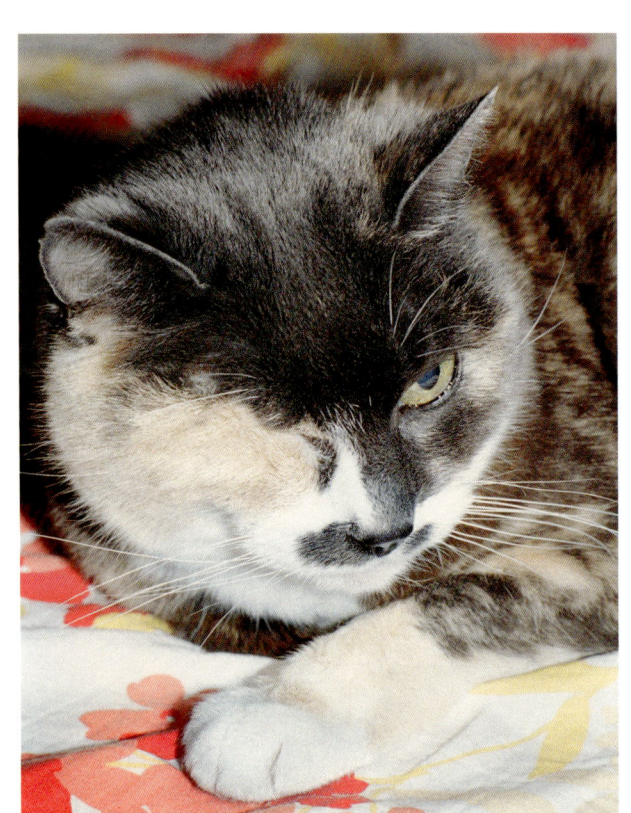

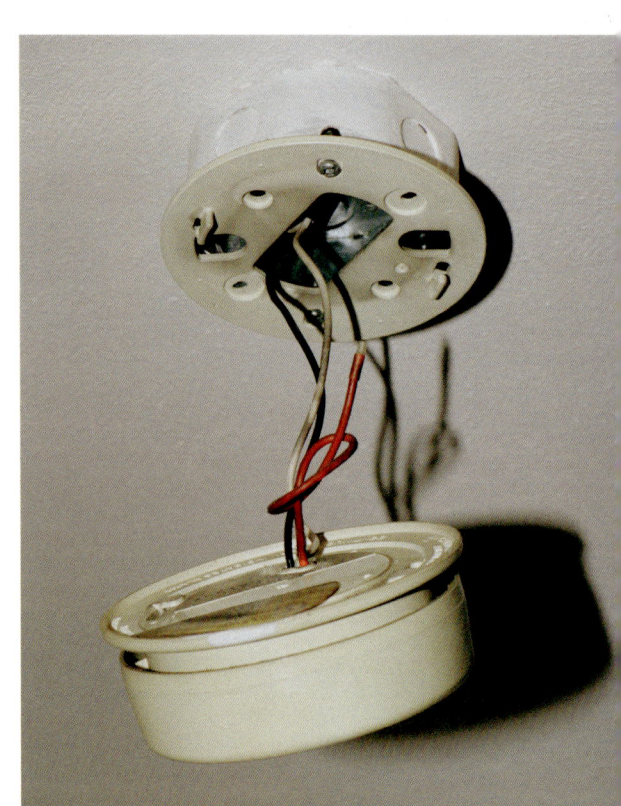

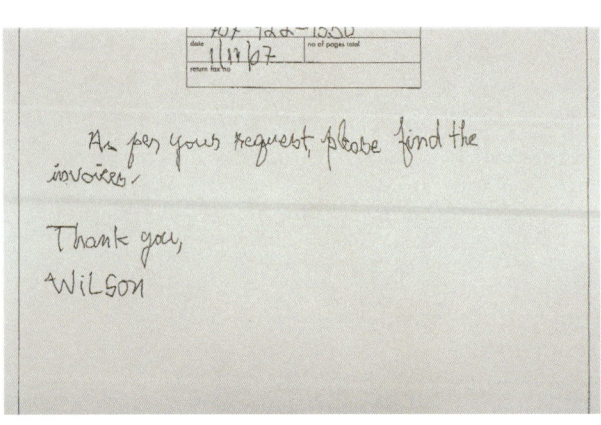

As per your request, please find the invoices.

Thank you,
WILSON

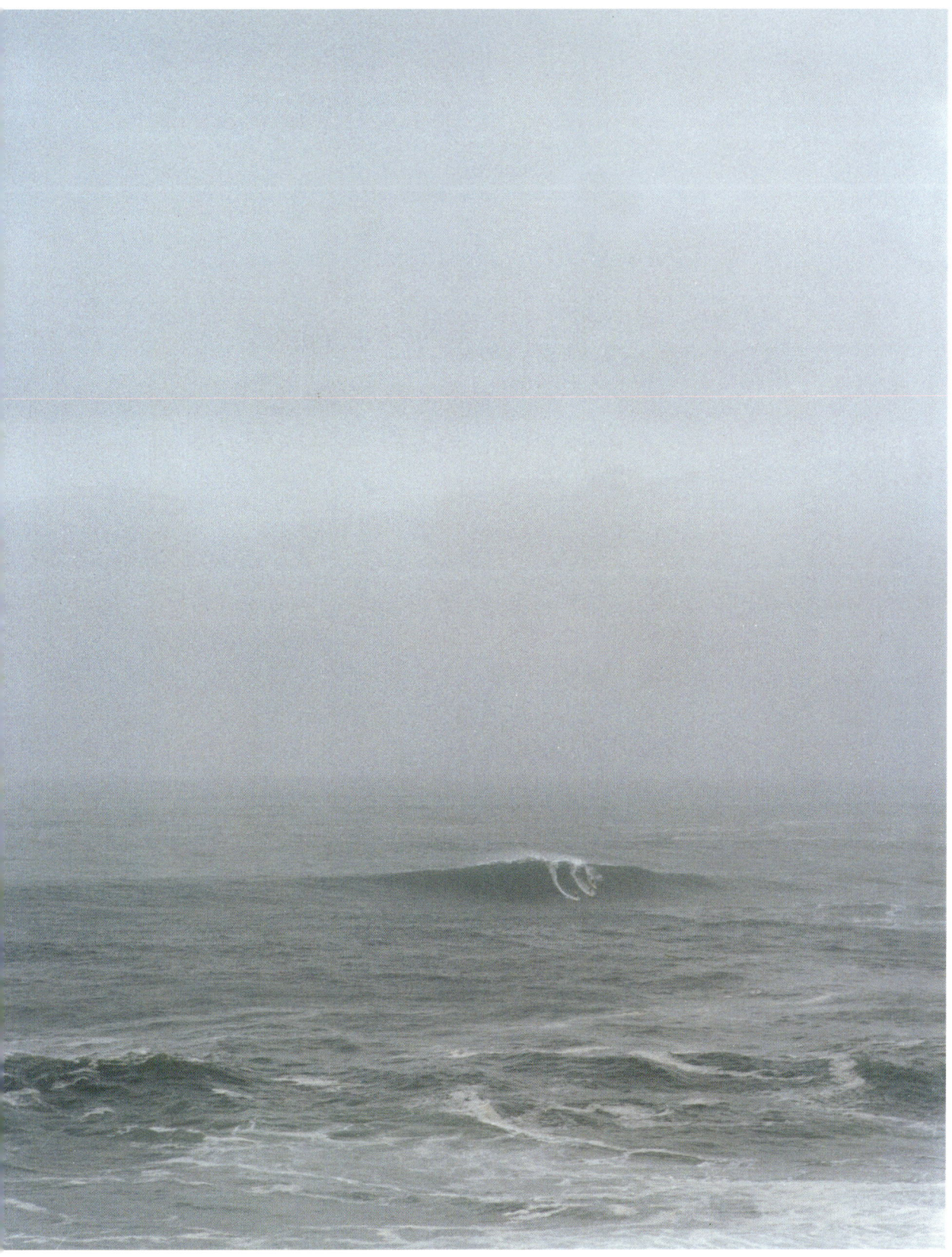

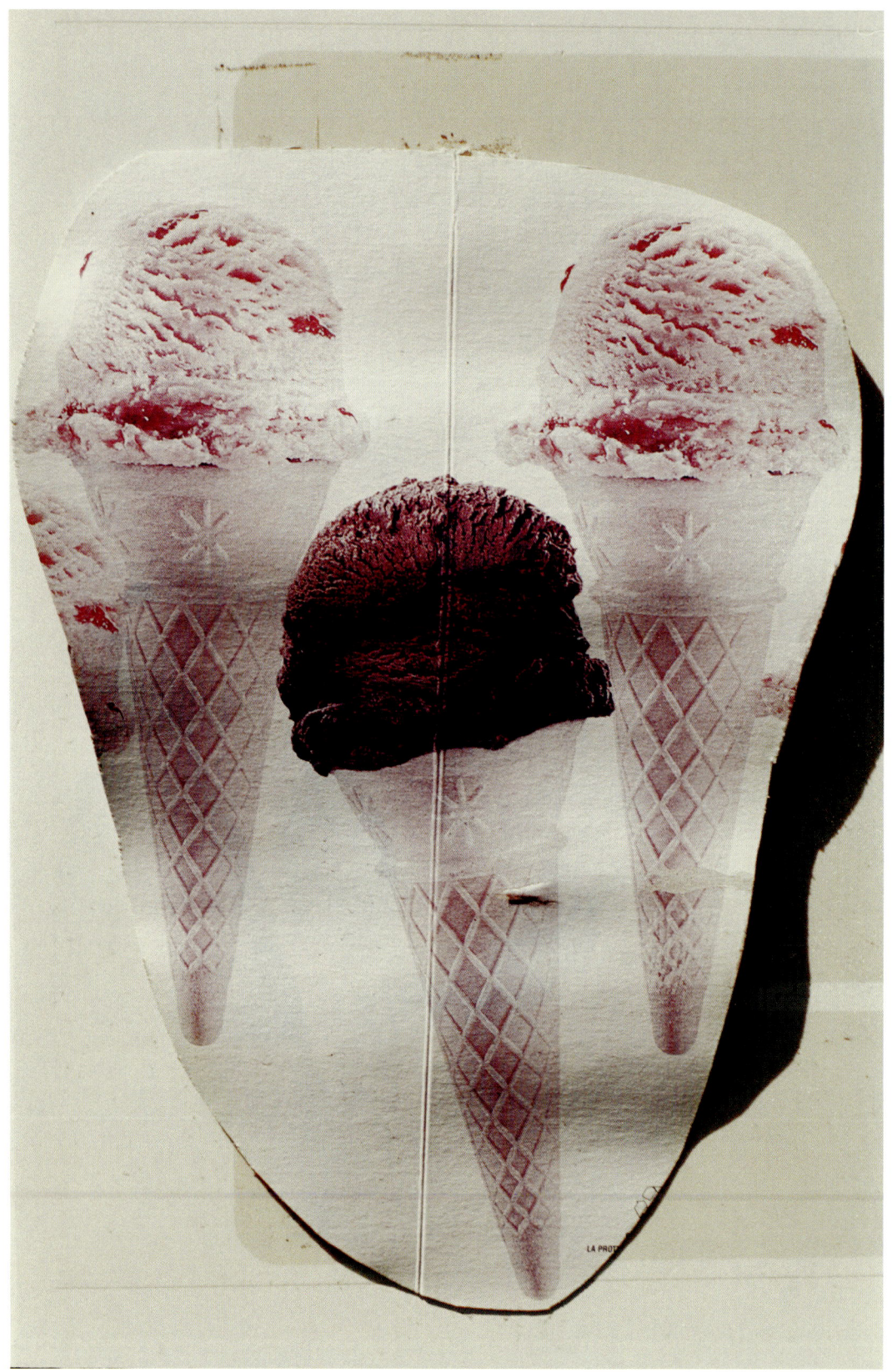

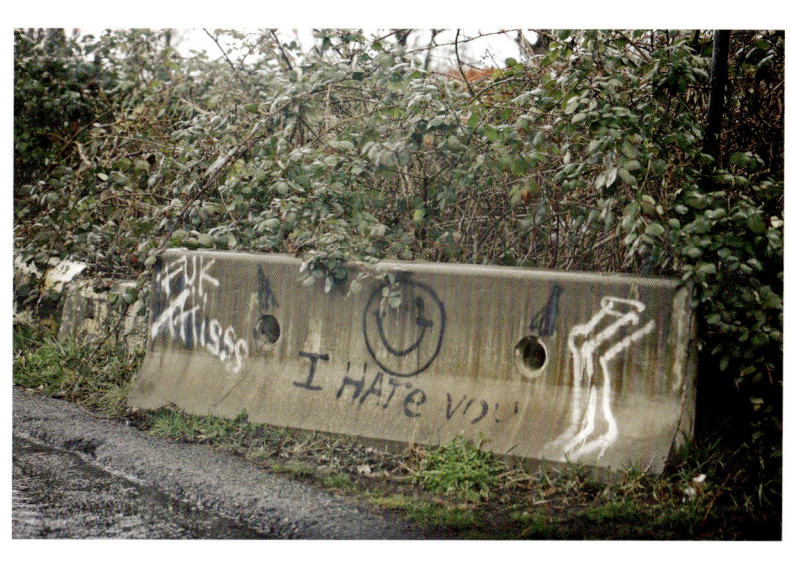

ACKNOWLEDGMENTS

Special thanks to: Meghan Lynch(soooooner foreverr), Tim, Ali,
Kuo, Kay, Brian, Pascal, Kelly, Sarah, John, Johnny, Anton, Will, Alex,
Wildman, Ted, Virgil, Elizabeth, Su, AJ, Tilly, Lumia, Marco, Dad,
Mom, Way, Bob, Adam, Stacey, The Lynchs, Tom Caravaglia, Deb,
Phil Bicker, Jeff Threats, Andre Dione and Lake.

Edited and designed by Tim Barber
Aperture Editor: Michael Famighetti
Publisher: Lesley A. Martin
Production: Matthew Pimm
Work Scholar: Carolyn Deuschle

Edition of 1,000
Printed in Singapore

Library of Congress Control Number: 2008928794
ISBN 978-1-59711-083-9

Aperture Foundation books are available in North America through:
D.A.P./Distributed Art Publishers
155 Sixth Avenue, 2nd Floor, New York, N.Y. 10013
Phone: (212) 627-1999, Fax: (212) 627-9484

Aperture Foundation books are distributed outside North America by:
Thames & Hudson
181A High Holborn, London WC1V 7QX, United Kingdom
Phone: + 44 20 7845 5000, Fax: + 44 20 7845 5055
Email: sales@thameshudson.co.uk

aperturefoundation

547 West 27th Street
New York, N.Y. 10001
www.aperture.org

The purpose of Aperture Foundation, a non-profit organization, is to
advance photography in all its forms and to foster the exchange of
ideas among audiences worldwide.